LIKE A WATERED GARDEN

QUOTES/INSIGHTS/REVELATIONS

FROM THE MINISTRY OF

Francis Frangipane

VOLUME ONE

LIKE A WATERED GARDEN

Unless otherwise indicated, Scripture is taken from the New American Standard Bible®, Copyright © 1960, 1962, 1963, 1968, 1971, 1972, 1973, 1975, 1977, 1995 by The Lockman Foundation. Used by permission.

Published by Arrow Publications, Inc.
P.O. Box 10102
Cedar Rapids, IA 52410

Ministry Resources/Books: Arrowbookstore.com

Teachings/Conferences: Frangipane.org

DEDICATION

At the request of friends and partners who have, over the years, requested I publish such a book of quotes, with humility, I dedicate this book to you.

INTRODUCTION

Welcome. I have called this journal *LIKE A WATERED GARDEN* for several reasons, the most important reason being that, no matter what condition in which I found myself – whether on a spiritual mountaintop or struggling through a dark and foreboding valley – in that very place the river of Christ's love has faithfully watered my soul. I testify to this great truth: my soul has been like a watered garden.

The metaphor of our being likened to a watered garden has another purpose: the Lord Himself has a unique affection for gardens. Remember, the first thing the Most High did after He established the principles of life on earth was to plant a garden. To me, this is a great thought, worthy of pause and reflection: *God planted a garden!* My imagination fails me.

However, Scripture also tells us that a river watered this first garden (Gen. 2:10). Humankind began the journey of life in a watered garden. Consider also that our Savior spent the night prior to His arrest praying in the Garden of Gethsemane: a place "He often met with His disciples" (John 18:2). From there He was buried in a garden tomb, and when He rose, He appeared to Mary, again in this same garden tomb.

What I am saying here is that the Lord's actions reveal a certain attraction to a garden devoted to Him. The first Adam began life in a garden; the second Adam, Christ, consummated a new Genesis in Christ's death, burial and resurrection – which also had its start in a garden.

Our Father put Adam into the garden to cultivate it. Likewise, God plants the seed of Christ in our hearts, but we too, working together with God, must cultivate the holy gift of Christ growing in us (Luke 8:15).

Beloved, if we stay with our great endeavor, our souls will increasingly become the Garden of God, planted and watered by our Father, a veritable Eden of virtue whose waters do not run dry.

—FRANCIS FRANGIPANE

LIKE A WATERED GARDEN

"And the Lord will
continually guide you,
And satisfy your desire
in scorched places,
And give strength to your bones;
And you will be
like a watered garden,
And like a spring of water
whose waters do not fail."

–ISAIAH 58:11–

BRINGING HEAVEN

The faith Christ inspires

not only brings us

to Heaven when we die,

but it is capable of

bringing Heaven

to where we live.

—In Christ's Image Training

NOTES/SCRIPTURES/DATE

_____

_____

_____

_____

_____

NO OTHER VIRTUE

Humility is the first of all virtues
and the sustainer of each.
No other virtue enters our souls
except humility first bids it come.
Indeed, no virtue attains its potential
except humility inspires its reach.
If our spiritual growth is truly a gift
of grace, then we must remember:
God gives grace only to the humble.

—IN CHRIST'S IMAGE TRAINING

NOTES/SCRIPTURES/DATE

_____

_____

_____

_____

YOUR OWN SOUL

Beware that you do not become

so consumed with the deteriorating

condition of the world that you

fail to notice the deteriorating

condition of your own soul.

—THIS DAY WE FIGHT!

NOTES/SCRIPTURES/DATE

_____

_____

_____

REVENGE

I heard Francis say this on TBN Television!

Bitterness is unfulfilled revenge.

—THE THREE BATTLEGROUNDS

NOTES/SCRIPTURES/DATE

_____

_____

_____

12

INOCULATED

I will never forget the day I realized that both God and the devil wanted me to die but for different reasons. Satan wanted to destroy me through slander while the Lord wanted to use those same lies to crucify my vulnerability to man's control. The Lord knew a time would come when my books would bless many people. So to inoculate me against the praise of man, He baptized me in the criticisms of man until I died to the opinions of man. Yes, I am accountable, but I now live only for God's pleasure. Whether I please or offend man, that is the Lord's business, not mine.

—THE SHELTER OF THE MOST HIGH

NOTES/SCRIPTURES/DATE

_____

_____

_____

_____

THE CROSSROAD

At some phase, each of us will be confronted with the impurities of our hearts. The Holy Spirit reveals our sinfulness not to condemn us but to establish humility and deepen the knowledge of our need for grace. It is at this crossroad that both holy men and hypocrites are bred. Those who become holy see their need and fall prostrate before God for deliverance. Those who become hypocrites are they who, in seeing their sin, excuse it and thus remain intact. Though all men must eventually stand at this juncture, few are they who embrace the voice of truth; few are they indeed who will walk humbly toward true holiness.

—HOLINESS, TRUTH AND THE PRESENCE OF GOD

NOTES/SCRIPTURES/DATE

_____

_____

_____

LIFE OR DEATH

We are deluged with information. News of disasters in lands previously unknown pours into our souls; wars with graphic photos flood our consciousness. The burden of the world's suffering exceeds our capacity to ingest it; our hearts harden in self-defense. And we are overstocked with fears. We have eaten from the Tree of Knowledge and it is killing us. Let us fast from the Tree of Knowledge and eat again from the Tree of Life. Find God, little flock. Find God.

—In Christ's Image Training

NOTES/SCRIPTURES/DATE

_____

_____

_____

THOUGHT LIFE

You will remember that the location where Jesus was crucified was called Golgotha, which meant "the place of the skull." If we will be effective in spiritual warfare, the first field of conflict where we must learn warfare is the battleground of the mind, i.e., "the place of the skull." For the territory of the uncrucified thought life is the beachhead of satanic assault in our lives.

—THE THREE BATTLEGROUNDS

NOTES/SCRIPTURES/DATE

_____

_____

_____

_____

_____

TOO LITTLE

Clearly, we think too much
and thank too little.

—IN CHRIST'S IMAGE TRAINING

NOTES/SCRIPTURES/DATE

_____

_____

_____

THANKFUL HEART

The thankful heart sees the best part
of every situation. It sees problems
and weaknesses as opportunities,
struggles as refining tools,
and sinners as saints in progress.

—IN CHRIST'S IMAGE TRAINING

NOTES/SCRIPTURES/DATE

_____

_____

_____

HEART RADAR

There's something like radar inside the human heart that senses the displeasure of others. Displeasure and ingratitude are like a repellent to human relationships. People think, "If you can't see anything good in me, I'll go where people will accept me as I am." This is especially true with our teenage children. Therefore, be thankful for your loved ones and tell them so. They don't have to be perfect for you to acknowledge the good you see in them. Acknowledge the good things often.

—IN CHRIST'S IMAGE TRAINING

NOTES/SCRIPTURES/DATE

_____

_____

_____

_____

_____

I WILL SURELY GIVE

A great rebellion against the Lord is unfolding before our eyes. Biblical standards are being mocked and replaced; perversity moves center stage. It is the new normal. Yet it is while rulers take "their stand ... against the Lord" (Ps. 2:2) that the Father tells His Son: "Ask of Me, and I will surely give [these very] nations as Your inheritance." Therefore, in spite of hell's advance, this day we ask God for our nations! Yes, we ask in faith, for God Himself has promised to give "the very ends of the earth as [Christ's] possession" (Ps. 2:8)!

—THIS DAY WE FIGHT!

NOTES/SCRIPTURES/DATE

_____

_____

_____

_____

REPENTANCE

John the Baptist, as the Messiah's forerunner, was sent to immerse Israel in an attitude of repentance (Acts 19:4). Historians estimate that over 750,000 people came to the wilderness to hear the prophet John; they came to repent and be baptized. Scripture says that John's task was to "prepare" and "make ready the way of the Lord" (Mark 1:2-3). Let's be sure we understand: repentance does not merely make men sorry; it makes men ready.

—HOLINESS, TRUTH AND THE PRESENCE OF GOD

NOTES/SCRIPTURES/DATE

_____

_____

_____

_____

THE RANSOM

Your soul was ransomed.

Your life was redeemed.

No matter what trap

holds you captive

or what dire scene

confronts you, there is

a rescue party coming,

and the Ransom for your release

leads the way.

—IN CHRIST'S IMAGE TRAINING

NOTES/SCRIPTURES/DATE

_____

_____

_____

_____

NO GREATER NEWS!

The fact that the Son of God Himself died for our sins reveals our extreme value to our Father. Would Jesus shed His blood to redeem what is worthless? Christ's death proves there is no price God would not pay for His children. Other religions provide moral codes and rituals; Christ provides Himself as the payment for our sins. There is no greater news in the universe!

—In Christ's Image Training

NOTES/SCRIPTURES/DATE

_____

_____

_____

_____

_____

MAKE OUR ABODE WITH HIM

Jesus answered

and said to him,

"If anyone loves Me,

he will keep My word;

and My Father will love him,

and We will come to him

and make Our abode with him."

–JOHN 14:23–

NOTES/SCRIPTURES/DATE

_____

_____

_____

_____

_____

OUR OBJECTIVE

It is easy to find fault and do nothing. The fact is all people are flawed, all churches have issues and entire cities, even nations, can backslide. The goal for us is not whether we can see what is wrong – that's important, but it's not the goal. Our objective is to look in the face of what is wrong and persevere in love and prayer until that which is wrong is made right.

—IN CHRIST'S IMAGE TRAINING

NOTES/SCRIPTURES/DATE

_____

_____

_____

_____

_____

END OF THE WORLD

People are worried, fearful that the world is soon coming to an end. Listen, for me as a Christian, the "end of the world" occurred the day I gave my life to Jesus Christ.

"But may it never be that I would boast, except in the cross of our Lord Jesus Christ, through which the world has been crucified to me, and I to the world" (Gal. 6:14).

—In Christ's Image Training

NOTES/SCRIPTURES/DATE

_____

_____

_____

_____

JUST OBEDIENT

The book of Acts says that Moses was educated in all the learning of the Egyptians, "a man of power in words and deeds" (Acts 7:22). Yet when God called him, Moses resisted, complaining that he was afflicted with a "slow ... tongue" and, as a man with a stutter, had "never been eloquent" (Exod. 4:10). Perhaps Moses just started stuttering when God said, "I'm going to send you." Is it possible that the speech impediment was God's idea – a "gift" given during his years in the desert, lest Moses feel he was chosen for his skills as an orator? For those who say, I'm too young or too old or uneducated to be used by God, I say, "That excuse is your stutter." You see, God does not need you to be eloquent, just obedient.

—IN CHRIST'S IMAGE TRAINING

NOTES/SCRIPTURES/DATE

_____

_____

_____

UNATTENDED VERSES

How sincere are we to know the heart of Christ? If you want to test your commitment as a disciple, try this: Open your Bible to the Gospels (anywhere will do). Do you see where you underlined or highlighted certain commands that Jesus taught? Now look at the other teachings, those that you didn't underline. These unattended verses represent aspects of Christ's nature and teaching where we are spiritually deficient. Minimizing them is one reason there isn't more power in our lives.

—In Christ's Image Training

NOTES/SCRIPTURES/DATE

_____

_____

_____

_____

HOW HE LOVES US

The great command – that we love God with all our heart, mind, soul and strength – intimidated me as a child. Yet, as I've come to know the Lord, I see that the reason He calls us to such a complete and unreserved love is because this is how He loves us. You see, to the degree we have been loved, so we will love. Our love is the consequence of His love (1 John 4:19).

—IN CHRIST'S IMAGE TRAINING

NOTES/SCRIPTURES/DATE

_____

_____

_____

_____

TEMPTATION

When the enemy first presents temp-tation, he promises that sin will feel like Heaven – that it will be worth the cost. However, what may have felt a little like "Heaven" in the beginning, over time degrades into the bondage of hell. In contrast, when the Holy Spirit calls us to deny ourselves and resist temptation, in the beginning it may feel a little like hell. However, in time, holding to the righ-teousness of God will unfold into Heaven.

—IN CHRIST'S IMAGE TRAINING

NOTES/SCRIPTURES/DATE

_____

_____

_____

_____

_____

YOU BE THE MAN

Some have lamented, "Where are the leaders who seek God?" Their complaint reminds me of a time in the 1980s when none of the city pastors attended our corporate morning prayer time. Alone in a cold, dark, unfamiliar church, I, too, lamented for nearly an hour. Suddenly the atmosphere changed. Everything – the hum of the furnace, the clatter of the grates, even my thoughts – all things were subdued. The presence of the Lord was in the room. Looking directly at me, He said, "You be the man you want the others to be." At that moment I stopped criticizing church leaders and started to become one.

—IN CHRIST'S IMAGE TRAINING

NOTES/SCRIPTURES/DATE

_____

_____

_____

TO WALK BY FAITH

We come to Christ and a new day begins. Yet the Lord's Day begins at evening, not morning (Gen. 1:5). It is here, as evening turns to night, that God teaches us to walk by faith. It is in this place – where we can hear but cannot see – that we learn to trust the promises of God. Dawn will come, beloved. When it does you will see that it was during the night that the Holy Spirit made you a true person of faith. The word He whispered to you in the darkness, that living word that saved you as you held it fast, you will proclaim in the light (Matt. 10:27). For what changed you will change others also.

—IN CHRIST'S IMAGE TRAINING

NOTES/SCRIPTURES/DATE

_____

_____

_____

TRAPPED IN MISERY

How easy it is to blame others
for our abiding unhappiness,
but we are only trapped in misery
when some thing or someone
other than Christ has become our life.

—IN CHRIST'S IMAGE TRAINING

NOTES/SCRIPTURES/DATE

_____

_____

_____

WEARINESS

If Satan cannot distract you

with worldliness, he will seek to

drain you with weariness.

—IN CHRIST'S IMAGE TRAINING

NOTES/SCRIPTURES/DATE

_____

_____

_____

ONE CORRECT ANSWER

Regardless of the nature of our tests, in spite of the circumstances surrounding them, there is one correct answer for every test we face: become like Jesus in the test. Once the devil sees that what he was using to defeat you is now being redeemed by God to perfect you – if instead of becoming bitter when offended, you appropriate more love or more faith – the devil will retreat. Become like Jesus in the test, and you will pass your test.

—In Christ's Image Training

NOTES/SCRIPTURES/DATE

_____

_____

_____

_____

_____

THE GLORY OF GOD

Beloved, today the Lord seeks to awaken you to His presence. Indeed, His promises are more than dreamlike realities reserved only for the hereafter. In this life, Moses lived in the glory of God; while still earthbound, Israel's elders "ate and drank" in the visible glory of God (Exod. 24:9-11). "Beholding ... the glory of the Lord" is a primary means of our transformation (2 Cor. 3:18)! Thus, if we want Christ to manifest through us, we must rouse ourselves from the opiates of worldliness and lethargy.

—THE DAYS OF HIS PRESENCE

NOTES/SCRIPTURES/DATE

_____

_____

_____

_____

_____

FEAR NOT

For I the Lord

thy God

will hold thy right hand,

saying unto thee,

Fear not;

I will help thee.

–Isaiah 41:13 kjv–

NOTES/SCRIPTURES/DATE

_____

_____

_____

_____

_____

PRAYER-MENTAL

Our call is to be a house of prayer for all nations. Consider the phrase "prayer for." Jesus instructed us to "pray for" those who mistreat us. When Job "prayed for" his friends, God restored him. Again, we are to "pray for" the peace of Jerusalem and "pray for" each other to be healed. Paul says God desires all men to be saved, thus "prayers ... [should] be made on behalf of all men ... and all who are in authority" (1 Tim. 2:1–2). In truth, God does not want us judge-mental – He wants us prayer-mental.

—THE POWER OF ONE CHRISTLIKE LIFE

NOTES/SCRIPTURES/DATE

_____

_____

_____

_____

_____

A PLACE FOR HIM

God asks for nothing but ourselves. Our beautiful church buildings, our slick professionalism, all are peripheral to the vision of God. The Most High does not want what we have; He wants who we are. He seeks to create in our hearts a sanctuary for Himself, a place where He may rest.

—HOLINESS, TRUTH AND THE PRESENCE OF GOD

NOTES/SCRIPTURES/DATE

_____

_____

_____

_____

_____

THE GAP

You do not need great discernment to find fault with the world around you. If you recall, you could find fault with life even before you were saved. But if you want to be like Christ, you must learn to be an intercessor, one who "stand[s] in the gap" (Ezek. 22:30). What is the gap? It's the distance between the way things are and the way things could be if God answered your prayers. You stand in that envisioned yet unformed reality and pray for mercy, for forgiveness and for redemption to flood the area of need!

—THE THREE BATTLEGROUNDS

NOTES/SCRIPTURES/DATE

_____

_____

_____

_____

_____

ALTER TO ALTAR

Although we cannot alter the past, we can put our past upon the altar.

—I WILL BE FOUND BY YOU

NOTES/SCRIPTURES/DATE

_____

_____

_____

ONE STEP CLOSER

Sin is addicting. Thus, we should beware when we casually, continually sin without any regret or remorse. Indeed, every time we choose the passing pleasures of sin we take one step closer to being given over to them (Rom. 1:21-28).

—IN CHRIST'S IMAGE TRAINING

NOTES/SCRIPTURES/DATE

_____

_____

_____

A RADIANT COUNTENANCE

It is not difficult to recognize one who has spent extended time at a newsstand: his conversation overflows with the drama of current news. And it is not hard to discern a person who has come from a sporting event, as his face reveals the outcome of the game. Likewise, others can tell when an individual has spent extended time seeking God. An imperturbable calm guards their heart, and their countenance is radiant with the morning dew of Heaven.

—I WILL BE FOUND BY YOU

NOTES/SCRIPTURES/DATE

_____

_____

_____

_____

_____

HE DESIRES YOU

The Lord desires

to increasingly become

as real, as full

and as all-consuming to you

as the world was

when you were

a sinner.

—In Christ's Image Training

NOTES/SCRIPTURES/DATE

_____

_____

_____

_____

_____

PURE GOLD

Like prospectors of old, you must stake your claim high in the Kingdom of God, being ready to defend your rights to the "pure gold" of Heaven (Rev. 3:18 TLB). And as you pitch your tent at the throne of grace, something eternal will begin to glow in you, like hot coals on a furnace floor. As you persist in faith, the sacred fire of God's presence will consume the wood, hay and stubble of your former ways. Power such as Jesus had will reside in your inner being. Angels will stand in awe, for your gold will be refined, your garments light, and your life holy.

—HOLINESS, TRUTH AND THE PRESENCE OF GOD

NOTES/SCRIPTURES/DATE

_____

_____

_____

_____

_____

SPEAK LIFE

Guard what you say, especially today. Yes, guard your tongue. Blessings await you but so also do self-induced troubles. Remember: life and death are in the power of your tongue. Indeed, James warns that the tongue "sets on fire the course of our life, and is set on fire by hell" (James 3:6). Don't destroy your life by speaking loveless words, for to do so is to sow into reality seeds of death. Speak life – reap life.

—IN CHRIST'S IMAGE TRAINING

NOTES/SCRIPTURES/DATE

_____

_____

_____

_____

THE DIVIDER

The short definition of the word *devil* is "slanderer." Yet literally speaking, the word refers to "one who puts himself or some thing between two in order to divide them." Satan's goal is not just to speak evil but to divide spouse from spouse, children from parents, race from race, and Christian from Christian. He will use unresolved issues from the past or even issues we may have already forgiven. The means to overcome is to make sure your heart is free of bitterness and your words are full of love; love covers a multitude of sins.

—A HOUSE UNITED

NOTES/SCRIPTURES/DATE

_____

_____

_____

_____

_____

SEARCH ME

David prayed, "Search me, O God, and know my heart; try me and know my anxious thoughts; and see if there be any hurtful way in me" (Ps. 139:23–24). Most are content to pray just the first part, "Search me, O God," but the true test of our repentance is when we pray "[and] try me." You see, David asked the Lord not just to forgive and change him but then to test those changes with situations that previously would have triggered an ungodly response. In essence, he prays, "Lord, verify that the work You've done in me is deep and unshakeable, that I am free even of any anxious thoughts about my previous vulnerability."

—In Christ's Image Training

NOTES/SCRIPTURES/DATE

_____

_____

_____

_____

_____

WHAT IS MAN?

Do you not know that we are the temple of the living God and that the Spirit of the Most High actually dwells within us (2 Cor. 6:16)? In this light, let us ask ourselves again the age-old question, "What is man?" We know how we appear to other men, but if God truly is within us, how do we appear to angels or devils? What light marks us in the spirit world, what illumination manifests through us, declaring to the invisible realm, "Behold and beware, here walks a son or daughter of God"? Think of it: the Spirit of the Creator, who purposed in the beginning to make man in His image, is in you ... now.

—HOLINESS, TRUTH AND THE PRESENCE OF GOD

NOTES/SCRIPTURES/DATE

_____

_____

_____

_____

DESTINED TO BE CHRISTLIKE

And we know that God causes
all things to work together for good
to those who love God,
to those who are called
according to His purpose.
For those whom He foreknew,
He also predestined to become
conformed to the image of His Son,
so that He would be the firstborn
among many brethren.
–ROMANS 8:28-29–

NOTES/SCRIPTURES/DATE

_____

_____

_____

_____

THE PAST IS IN US

We've heard, and even valued the counsel, "Leave it in the past." It is advice that promises we can unburden our minds of grievous pain or loss. Yet where is the past that I might leave my sorrows there? Is the past in some ethereal realm? The truth is, we cannot leave the past, for the past is in us; it is in our mind and heart. For some, it is a place of torment, where "specters [haunt] the scene of past transgressions" (Prov. 9:18 AMP). Yet our souls can be renewed. The issues of the past can be brought to Christ. We cannot leave the past, but it can be forgiven, released and redeemed.

—IN CHRIST'S IMAGE TRAINING

NOTES/SCRIPTURES/DATE

_____

_____

_____

_____

HEART FULL OF LOVE

What fills the heart cannot long be hidden. When the heart is expanded by love, are not the affections of love revealed in its many encouragements and concerns? Its joy is unabashed in loving its beloved. Bitterness, too, cannot be hidden. However, a bitter soul is not seeking healing but justice. Its passion is driven by the unresolved theft of its peace, personhood or possessions. A bitter soul is conjoined to the injustice committed against it. Thus, it is perpetually reminded of the pain and perpetually wounded. *To forgive is to be released from the pain of the past.*

—In Christ's Image Training

NOTES/SCRIPTURES/DATE

_____

_____

_____

_____

_____

HE WILL CONFRONT US

Paul was a man who trusted in his religious pedigree: a Pharisee of Pharisees of the tribe of Benjamin, etc. (Phil. 3:4–6). Yet, until the Lord confronted him on the road to Damascus, these outward things masked his true nature. Confronted by Christ, Paul not only saw God's glory, he saw his own utter sinfulness. His opinion of himself was crushed; his outer man, broken. We too are on a journey. We too mask our true nature. Yet a time will come when, in His mercy, the Lord will confront us as He confronted Paul. He will meet us on the road to de-mask-us.

—In Christ's Image Training

NOTES/SCRIPTURES/DATE

_____

_____

_____

A HEART AFTER GOD

Today many pine away. It is obvious to me: the great need of Christians is for more of God. As it was written, "God has looked down from heaven upon the sons of men to see if there is anyone who understands, who seeks after God" (Ps. 53:2). Do we grasp this? Seeking God – possessing a heart after God – this is the key that unlocks everything.

—I WILL BE FOUND BY YOU

NOTES/SCRIPTURES/DATE

_____

_____

_____

_____

_____

BATTLES DRAG ON

There are many reasons

Satan is called the "dragon,"

not the least of which

is his ability

to cause battles and delays

to "drag on."

—IN CHRIST'S IMAGE TRAINING

NOTES/SCRIPTURES/DATE

_____

_____

_____

_____

_____

GOOD SOIL

We must cooperate with God. The Word says, in effect, that we work out what God is working in us (Phil. 2:12–13). Indeed, Jesus described "good soil" as that which bears fruit "with perseverance" (Luke 8:15). Paul said we will "reap, if we faint not" (Gal. 6:9 KJV). Consider wisely: we can have the best soil and sow the most perfect seed, but if we faint we will not reap.

—IN CHRIST'S IMAGE TRAINING

NOTES/SCRIPTURES/DATE

_____

_____

_____

_____

_____

INDIGNATION

We can be legitimately angry

about things that

are absolutely wrong,

but at some point

our indignation

must climb to a more noble,

redemptive expression.

—IN CHRIST'S IMAGE TRAINING

NOTES/SCRIPTURES/DATE

_____

_____

_____

_____

_____

THE MAIN REASON

Perhaps the main reason
the devil doesn't fear the church
is because the church
doesn't fear the Lord.

—IN CHRIST'S IMAGE TRAINING

NOTES/SCRIPTURES/DATE

_____

_____

_____

TO COMPLETE

The church was not created
to fulfill God's wrath
but to complete His mercy.

—THE POWER OF ONE CHRISTLIKE LIFE

NOTES/SCRIPTURES/DATE

_____

_____

_____

CAPTIVE?

Our Father wants us to learn
from our failures,
not be held captive to them.

—IN CHRIST'S IMAGE TRAINING

NOTES/SCRIPTURES/DATE

_____

_____

_____

TILL WE PASS THEM

We don't really fail the tests
of God – He just keeps giving us
the same ones till we pass them.

—IN CHRIST'S IMAGE TRAINING

NOTES/SCRIPTURES/DATE

_____

_____

_____

OFFENDED

We pray, "Lord, change me." To answer that prayer, He will often allow circumstances or people to offend us. Our fleshly reaction spotlights the specific area where we need growth. Thus, the Lord initiates change by offending the area of our soul He seeks to transform. He does not expect us to merely survive this adversity but become Christlike in it.

—IN CHRIST'S IMAGE TRAINING

NOTES/SCRIPTURES/DATE

_____

_____

_____

_____

THE EXCHANGE

In our anxious, stress-filled world, we must find the rest of God. Yet we are not associating God's rest merely with the sense of being rebuilt or rejuvenated, which we obviously need and associate with human rest. The rest we seek is not a rejuvenation of our energy; it is the exchange of energy: our life for God's. It is this divine rest that we seek, where the vessel of our humanity is filled with the divine presence and the all-sufficiency of Christ Himself.

—HOLINESS, TRUTH AND THE PRESENCE OF GOD

NOTES/SCRIPTURES/DATE

_____
_____
_____
_____
_____

WILL IT SUFFICE?

As the pressures of this age
escalate, we will soon discover
that yesterday's anointing
will not suffice for today's battles.

—THE SHELTER OF THE MOST HIGH

NOTES/SCRIPTURES/DATE

_____

_____

_____

GIVE OVER

What you give over,

God will take over.

—IN CHRIST'S IMAGE TRAINING

NOTES/SCRIPTURES/DATE

_____

_____

_____

TO THIS ONE I WILL LOOK

Thus says the Lord, "Heaven is My throne

and the earth is My footstool.

Where then is a house

you could build for Me?

And where is a place that I may rest?

For My hand made all these things,

thus all these things came into being,"

declares the Lord.

"But to this one I will look,

To him who is humble and contrite

of spirit, and who trembles at My word."

–Isaiah 66:1-2–

NOTES/SCRIPTURES/DATE

_____

_____

_____

A STRONGHOLD

Let's take a moment today and survey the landscape of your heart. Every area in your thinking that glistens with hope in God's transforming work is an area being liberated by Christ. But any system of thinking that is guarded by hopelessness – that feels like it will never improve – this is a stronghold that is oppressing you. Identify it, repent for allowing it, and take faith for your mind to be renewed in the precise area where you were oppressed. God will help you.

—THE THREE BATTLEGROUNDS

NOTES/SCRIPTURES/DATE

_____

_____

_____

_____

HUMBLE HEART

The greatest defense
we can have against the devil
is to maintain an honest and
humble heart before the Lord.

—THE THREE BATTLEGROUNDS

NOTES/SCRIPTURES/DATE

_____
_____
_____

BELIEVE LIKE HIM

It is one thing
to believe in Christ,
another thing to believe like Him.

—IN CHRIST'S IMAGE TRAINING

NOTES/SCRIPTURES/DATE

_____
_____
_____

GOD CAN MAKE A WAY

According to America's Foundation for Chess, there are 318,979,564,000 possible ways of playing the first four moves in chess. This tells me that no matter how dark our circumstances, if we will humble ourselves and keep faith in God, He can counter any move of the devil. We might not see a way, but God can make a way. For nothing is impossible with God!

—IN CHRIST'S IMAGE TRAINING

NOTES/SCRIPTURES/DATE

_____
_____
_____
_____
_____

THE DEVIL TREMBLES

Satan fears virtue. He is most terrified of humility; he hates it. He sees a humble person and it sends chills down his back. His hair stands up when Christians kneel down, for true humility is the surrender of the soul to God. The devil trembles before the meek because in the very areas where he once had access there stands the Lord, and Satan is terrified of Jesus Christ.

—THE THREE BATTLEGROUNDS

NOTES/SCRIPTURES/DATE

_____

_____

_____

_____

WHOSE SPIRIT?

Our words, manipulated by hell, can become weapons the enemy uses to destroy us and wound others. Recall Job's challenge to his so-called friends: "Whose spirit was expressed through you?" (Job 26:4). When we slander or gossip, let us discern the spirit that is being expressed through us. You see, we criticize but do not pray; we complain but do not trust God; we judge but without mercy, thus cutting ourselves off from access to the very mercy we ourselves so desperately need (James 2:13).

—IN CHRIST'S IMAGE TRAINING

NOTES/SCRIPTURES/DATE

_____

_____

_____

_____

_____

LIVING AND BREATHING

Some of my greatest times
with the Lord have been when
He manifests Himself
through the Scriptures.
At that moment the same Spirit
that hovered over creation
in the beginning
is hovering over my heart,
transforming me through the Word
into the image of Christ.

—IN CHRIST'S IMAGE TRAINING

NOTES/SCRIPTURES/DATE

_____

_____

_____

_____

PLANT THE SEED

If you desire to see

the reality of God reproduced

in your loved ones,

set your heart to walk in

the fruit of the Spirit.

The seed that empowers

spiritual reproduction is not found

in our religion but in our fruit.

—IN CHRIST'S IMAGE TRAINING

NOTES/SCRIPTURES/DATE

_____

_____

_____

_____

_____

67

TEACHER OR LORD?

During the most somber night of His life, Jesus warned His apostles that a betrayer was among them. Deeply grieved, each asked, "Surely not I, Lord?" Finally, Judas also answered, saying, "Surely it is not I, Rabbi?" (Matt. 26:20-25). Do we see this? The other disciples, though flawed, knew Jesus as their Lord. To them, Christ's words were commands, not just teachings. Judas, however, never accepted Jesus as Lord. The lordship of Christ never replaced the self-will of Judas. So let us ask ourselves: Are the words of Christ just casual thoughts or are they commands uttered by the Lord of Heaven?

—IN CHRIST'S IMAGE TRAINING

NOTES/SCRIPTURES/DATE

_____

_____

_____

_____

HIS INDWELLING

What we define doctrinally as "salvation" is, in truth, the entrance, and then expansion, of Christ's presence within us. As we accept Him, Christ unites with our spirit and begins His transformational work: He influences our thoughts, giving us insight into the Scriptures, convicting us of sin, and creating godly attitudes within us. He brings healing to the wounds of our past, and even our mortal bodies are quickened by His indwelling.

—IN CHRIST'S IMAGE TRAINING

NOTES/SCRIPTURES/DATE

_____

_____

_____

_____

_____

JESUS IS

Even in the most serious corrections, the voice of Jesus is always the embodiment of "grace and truth" (John 1:14).

—When the Many Are One

NOTES/SCRIPTURES/DATE

_____

_____

_____

ARMOR OF DARKNESS

God can never entrust His kingdom
to anyone who has not been
broken of pride;
pride is the armor of darkness itself.

—In Christ's Image Training

NOTES/SCRIPTURES/DATE

_____

_____

_____

OUR MINISTRY SOURCE

When Jesus began His ministry, He selected the twelve to be apostles. According to Mark's Gospel, our Lord's goal was, first of all, that these men "would be with Him" (Mark 3:14). Out of actually being with Him, the disciples would come to know Him and in knowing Him, represent Him. Likewise Jesus calls us, not only to believe in Him but to live our lives with Him. All ministry that flows outwardly to people comes as the overflow of a life lived inwardly with Jesus.

—IN CHRIST'S IMAGE TRAINING

NOTES/SCRIPTURES/DATE

_____

_____

_____

_____

_____

INTO THE SAME IMAGE

But we all, with unveiled face, beholding as in a mirror the glory of the Lord, are being transformed into the same image from glory to glory, just as from the Lord, the Spirit.

–2 CORINTHIANS 3:18–

NOTES/SCRIPTURES/DATE

_____

_____

_____

SELF

To advance in God we must retreat from self.

—IN CHRIST'S IMAGE TRAINING

NOTES/SCRIPTURES/DATE

_____

_____

_____

INTERCESSION

The primary reason for our existence is our conformity to Christ. But you cannot become Christlike without embracing intercession for others. Christ's whole life was one of intercession, from everything He taught to everything He did. Yes, He reproved His disciples when necessary. True, He confronted the hardness of the Pharisees' hearts. But the nectar of Christ's passion is seen when, from His cross, He prayed, "Father, forgive them." He interceded for the very people who mocked and killed Him and, by extension, all mankind.

—IN CHRIST'S IMAGE TRAINING

NOTES/SCRIPTURES/DATE

_____

_____

_____

_____

_____

PREPARED

The last great move of

the Holy Spirit will be

distinguished by men

and women

who have been prepared

by God for God.

—IN CHRIST'S IMAGE TRAINING

NOTES/SCRIPTURES/DATE

_____

_____

_____

_____

_____

74

RELIGIOUS SPIRIT

There is a difference between a religious spirit and the Spirit of God. A religious spirit is hollow, without life; the Spirit of God is holy, overflowing with life. Jesus rebuked the religious leaders of His day, saying, "You build the tombs of the prophets, and it was your fathers who killed them" (Luke 11:47). In other words, a religious spirit will honor what God has done while fighting what God is doing.

—IN CHRIST'S IMAGE TRAINING

NOTES/SCRIPTURES/DATE

_____

_____

_____

_____

_____

THE GOAL

The Holy Spirit is a mystery to most. Some believe His primary purpose is to give spiritual gifts; others believe He comes uniquely as a helper to comfort and guide. Still others see Him as one who convicts the world of sin, righteousness and judgment.

All of these are absolutely true, but none in itself represents the Spirit's consummate goal, which is to lead us into the manifest presence of Jesus Christ.

—IN CHRIST'S IMAGE TRAINING

NOTES/SCRIPTURES/DATE

_____

_____

_____

_____

_____

PRAYING MOTHERS

I know well the power of a mother's prayer. In the 1960s I was a very lost man. Yet my dear mom prayed unceasingly for me. Finally, divine power uniquely drawn by her prayers began to turn my heart until, in 1970, I came to Christ during the Jesus movement. Years later I asked the Lord about this revival. My assignment was to help inspire unity and prayer in the church, things which precede revival. Yet seemingly neither preceded the Jesus movement. "Lord," I asked, "how could revival occur without a prayer movement?" The Lord said that there was indeed a great prayer movement. He had answered the prayers of a million praying mothers crying out for their children.

—THIS DAY WE FIGHT!

NOTES/SCRIPTURES/DATE

_____

_____

_____

GRACE TO SEE

Spiritual discernment

is the grace to see

into the unseen.

It is a gift of the Spirit

to perceive the realm

of the spirit.

—THE THREE BATTLEGROUNDS

NOTES/SCRIPTURES/DATE

_____

_____

_____

_____

_____

FIX FOR REVIVAL

One issue keeping America

from experiencing

a national revival is this:

we are angry that the world

has not become Christian

while, at the same time,

we are complacent that

we've not become Christlike.

—In Christ's Image Training

NOTES/SCRIPTURES/DATE

_____

_____

_____

_____

_____

A LIVING SHELTER

As the day of Christ's return draws near, entrance into His glory shall not only become more attainable, it shall become more necessary. For as the end times intensify and just prior to the rapture of the church, the glory of God shall become a living shelter for His people. In His great love, His presence shall consume the chaff of our worldliness; our fears, which held us in bondage, shall dissolve into praise. What shall remain is a people purified and secure in the living fire of His presence (Isa. 4).

—IN CHRIST'S IMAGE TRAINING

NOTES/SCRIPTURES/DATE

_____

_____

_____

_____

_____

SIGNIFICANCE

One day we each will stand before the throne of God. At that time He will measure what we overcame and whether we used the gifts He gave us. More specifically, He will probe to see if we truly lived by faith and how steadfastly we served the cause of love and redemption. To the degree that Christ flourished in us in life, we will receive an eternal reward. Thus, I say, do not fret about your significance on earth. For the only words that truly matter will be those spoken by our Master: "Well done, good and faithful servant." It is in eternity that our significance will be established, and it will be set by the only view that matters.

—IN CHRIST'S IMAGE TRAINING

NOTES/SCRIPTURES/DATE

_____

_____

_____

TRUE GOD-SEEKERS

Beloved, loving God is not hard. We can fulfill any assignment – auto mechanic or housewife, doctor or college student – and still give great pleasure to our heavenly Father. We do not need ministry titles to love the Lord. Indeed, God measures the value of our lives by the depth of our love. This is what He requires of all true God-seekers: to love Him where we are at.

—I WILL BE FOUND BY YOU

NOTES/SCRIPTURES/DATE

_____

_____

_____

_____

_____

THE DRY BONES

The Lord showed Ezekiel a valley of dry bones and asked His prophet if the bones could live. The Lord did not send Ezekiel to criticize the bones or judge them for being lifeless. He told Ezekiel to *speak* to them and as he did, the bones came together to become an exceedingly great army – an army empowered by the wind of the Spirit. You see, God doesn't call us merely to criticize the dry bones. He tells us to speak life to them.

—WHEN THE MANY ARE ONE

NOTES/SCRIPTURES/DATE

_____

_____

_____

_____

HIS WORD

The scene is familiar: Peter is about to step out of the boat and walk on the water. Now I should clarify: Peter is not going to walk on the water, not really. When he steps out, he is walking on the Word spoken by Jesus: *"Come!"* Peter has repeatedly seen that the power to accomplish the impossible resides in Christ's Word, and it is upon the super-natural reality of the Word that Peter walks.

—THIS DAY WE FIGHT!

NOTES/SCRIPTURES/DATE

_____

_____

_____

_____

NEVER LANGUISH AGAIN

"They will come and shout for joy
on the height of Zion,
And they will be radiant
over the bounty of the Lord -
Over the grain and the new wine
and the oil,
And over the young of the flock
and the herd; and their life will be
like a watered garden,
And they will never languish again."
–JEREMIAH 31:12–

NOTES/SCRIPTURES/DATE

_____
_____
_____
_____
_____

FIRST A WORSHIPER

Let's make this clear:

David was first a worshiper of God.

He did not pursue his enemies

without first pursuing God.

Because he was first a worshiper,

when the Lord led him into war,

he thoroughly defeated his foes.

—THE SHELTER OF THE MOST HIGH

NOTES/SCRIPTURES/DATE

_____

_____

_____

_____

_____

JESUS – UNDILUTED

Look at what Jesus did with common men. In just three and one half years, average men and women were transformed into fearless disciples filled with the Holy Spirit! They did not wince at suffering nor withdraw from sacrifice. These ordinary souls received authority over demons and power over illnesses! They were proof that Christ transforms people. Three years of undiluted walking with Jesus can produce in us what He did in them.

—WHEN THE MANY ARE ONE

NOTES/SCRIPTURES/DATE

_____

_____

_____

_____

_____

TO LIBERATE

In the Kingdom of God,
the goal of those in authority is
not to dominate but to liberate.

—IN CHRIST'S IMAGE TRAINING

NOTES/SCRIPTURES/DATE

_____

_____

_____

NEED A SAVIOR

We do not need a Savior
only for what we do;
we need a Savior for what we are.

—IN CHRIST'S IMAGE TRAINING

NOTES/SCRIPTURES/DATE

_____

_____

_____

AS REAL AS YOUR LOVE

Is your love growing –
becoming softer, brighter,
more daring and more visible?
Or is it becoming
more discriminating, more calculating,
less vulnerable and less available?
This is a very important issue,
for your Christianity
is only as real as your love.

—THE THREE BATTLEGROUNDS

NOTES/SCRIPTURES/DATE

_____

_____

_____

_____

_____

HE COMES TO CLEANSE

We can be assured that each step
deeper into the Lord's presence
will reveal areas in our hearts
that need to be cleansed.
Do not be afraid to see yourself
as you are. For when
the Holy Spirit shows you your sin,
He comes not to condemn
but to cleanse and deliver.

—HOLINESS, TRUTH AND THE PRESENCE OF GOD

NOTES/SCRIPTURES/DATE

_____
_____
_____
_____
_____

CIRCUMSTANCES

If you are serious about

wanting to be like Christ,

He is going to

put you in circumstances

where your only true choice

is to become like Him.

—IN CHRIST'S IMAGE TRAINING

NOTES/SCRIPTURES/DATE

_____

_____

_____

_____

_____

EFFECTIVE STRATEGY

I've often been approached by church leaders or intercessors who ask for insight into the spiritual battle in their region. "What's the name of the spirit resisting the church in our area?" they ask. My reply: "The name of the Spirit opposing many Christians is Yahweh." They look puzzled until I bring up James 4:6, which says, "God is opposed to the proud, but gives grace to the humble." So, unless we humble ourselves, God will resist our prideful attitudes. We can engage in a variety of warfare techniques, but we can't cast out God. All effective strategies begin with God's people repenting of pride. As the Lord says, "If My people ... humble themselves" (2 Chron. 7:14 KJV).

—IN CHRIST'S IMAGE TRAINING

NOTES/SCRIPTURES/DATE

_____

_____

_____

WORSHIP IS

Prayer is an appeal to God
based on our needs
and the needs of our world.
Worship is not the articulation
of our needs;
it is the consummation
of our love.
Worship is what we offer to God
regardless of the status
of our needs.

—IN CHRIST'S IMAGE TRAINING

NOTES/SCRIPTURES/DATE

_____

_____

_____

_____

THE FRAGRANCE

While the Lord desires that we enjoy His gifts, He would have us know we were created first for His pleasure. At the end of this age, the Lord will have a people whose singular purpose for living is to please God. In them, God finds His own reward for creating man. They are His worshipers. The Lord takes them farther and through more conflicts than other men. Outwardly, they often seem "smitten of God, and afflicted" (Isa. 53:4). Yet they are beloved by God. When they are crushed, like the petals of a flower, they exude a worship, the fragrance of which is so beautiful and rare that angels weep in quiet awe at their surrender.

—THE THREE BATTLEGROUNDS

NOTES/SCRIPTURES/DATE

_____
_____
_____
_____

OUR GREATEST QUEST

Christian study guides

can be very helpful, and

training books can

enhance our walk with God.

Yet our greatest quest

is not to follow a manual

but to actually follow Emmanuel.

—IN CHRIST'S IMAGE TRAINING

NOTES/SCRIPTURES/DATE

_____

_____

_____

_____

_____

CHRIST IN ME

When God calls me to humble myself, it does not mean that I simply say to the Lord, "I humble myself." True humility goes farther; it is deeper. It means I see myself as a servant to others, not one above them (Mark 9:35). I also can confess my sins, even the darkest, to a trusted friend. The meekness I seek uproots my self-righteous instincts to judge others. Because I now see clearly my need of mercy, I pray for God's mercy to cover others (Matt. 5:7). I abandon my religious pretensions. And when God speaks, I tremble (Isa. 66:2).

You see, just saying "Lord, I humble myself" does not mean I have actually humbled myself. Not until Christ is enthroned in me where self once ruled will I possess true humility.

—IN CHRIST'S IMAGE TRAINING

NOTES/SCRIPTURES/DATE

_____

_____

_____

THIS ONE THING I DO

But whatever things were gain to me, those things I have counted as loss for the sake of Christ. More than that, I count all things to be loss in view of the surpassing value of knowing Christ Jesus my Lord, for whom I have suffered the loss of all things, and count them but rubbish so that I may gain Christ, and may be found in Him, not having a righteousness of my own derived from the Law, but that which is through faith in Christ, the righteousness which comes from God on the basis of faith, that I may know Him and the power of His resurrection and the fellowship of His sufferings, being conformed to His death; in order that I may attain to the resurrection from the dead.

—Philippians 3:7–11—

NOTES/SCRIPTURES/DATE

_____

_____

_____

HOLINESS AND POWER

Jesus lived for thirty years in sinless purity before He did one work of power. His life goal was not to do great works but to please God with a surrendered life. Likewise, our highest goal should not be to become powerful but to walk holy in the overflow of Christ's presence. God promises to empower those He first makes holy. Indeed, a mature Christian will be both holy and powerful, but holiness will precede power.

—HOLINESS, TRUTH AND THE PRESENCE OF GOD

NOTES/SCRIPTURES/DATE

_____

_____

_____

_____

_____

A LOVELESS HEART

Six times in Matthew 24 Jesus warned of rampant deception at the end of the age. Certainly, false prophets and false teachers are among us, and they are misleading many. Yes, we must zealously guard our doctrines, and with passion pursue the truth. Yet for all the heresy in our world, one form of deception goes almost unchecked in the church: the apostasy of a loveless heart. What value is it to possess right doctrines if our love for others has grown cold?

—IN CHRIST'S IMAGE TRAINING

NOTES/SCRIPTURES/DATE

_____

_____

_____

_____

_____

THE WAR MODE

The war mode is in us all. It is directly connected with our love. I love my nation so I am warring in prayer on its behalf. Because of love for my family, I war in prayer for their well-being. I love my church and my city and, of course, my own soul. I war to protect what I love. If there is a natural fight instinct, there is a spiritual fight mode as well. It just needs to be awakened, submitted to Christ, and then unleashed against the enemy. If you have a love mode, you also have a war mode. God has created the war mode so we can protect the people we love.

—THIS DAY WE FIGHT!

NOTES/SCRIPTURES/DATE

_____

_____

_____

_____

WITHHOLD NOTHING

You will remember that at the fall of man in the Garden of Eden, the judgment of God against the devil was that he should "eat dust." Remember also that God said of man, "dust thou art" (Gen. 3:14–19 KJV). The essence of our carnal nature – of all that is carnal in nature – is dust. We need to see the connection here: Satan feeds upon our earthly, carnal nature of "dust." Therefore, we must walk in the Spirit, withholding nothing from the presence of God.

—THE THREE BATTLEGROUNDS

NOTES/SCRIPTURES/DATE

_____

_____

_____

_____

WE MUST FIGHT

Jesus knew this world was a realm under satanic siege. Planet Earth was not a place of peace but a realm at war. From the casting out of Lucifer and his angels from Heaven, to the temptation in the Garden of Eden, to Babylon and the multiplication of nations under satanic influence, our world has been an embattled world. The idea that somehow our era is less threatened by evil is the height of deception. We must fight if we will follow Christ into victory.

—THIS DAY WE FIGHT!

NOTES/SCRIPTURES/DATE

_____

_____

_____

_____

HEALER'S HANDS

Hosea 6:1 tells us that God's hands
will, at times, wound before they heal.
He must cripple our self-confidence
so we can truly become
God-confident. He breaks and
empties us of pride so that we
who once were full of self
might instead be filled with Christ.

—IN CHRIST'S IMAGE TRAINING

NOTES/SCRIPTURES/DATE

_____

_____

_____

_____

_____

IN SPIRITUAL TRAVAIL

The intercessory prayer of the apostle Paul was not just for protection or for a few blessings to rest upon the church. He said, "My children, with whom I am again in labor until Christ is formed in you" (Gal. 4:19). Paul was in labor, in spiritual travail, to bring forth Christ within the church – not just Christianity but the full bloom of Christ in both character and power!

—IN CHRIST'S IMAGE TRAINING

NOTES/SCRIPTURES/DATE

_____

_____

_____

_____

FULL STATURE

Before Jesus Himself returns, the last virgin church shall become pregnant with the promise of God. Out of her travail the body of Christ shall mature and be raised to the full stature of its head, the Lord Jesus (Eph. 4:13). Corporately manifested in holiness, power and love, the bride of Christ shall arise clothed in white garments, bright and clean (Rev. 19:7-8).

—HOLINESS, TRUTH AND THE PRESENCE OF GOD

NOTES/SCRIPTURES/DATE

_____

_____

_____

_____

_____

AMAZING GRACE!

We sing "Amazing Grace," but do we truly realize how amazing grace actually is? Before we were spiritually reborn, grace was powerfully working in our hearts. Recall that Jesus said, "No one can come to Me unless the Father who sent Me draws him" (John 6:44). Do you remember that drawing power? Yet grace is more. For after Jesus spoke of the Father's drawing power, He then said, "And I will raise him up on the last day" (v. 44). This is the commitment of our Father's love: from our being utterly helpless in sin to being utterly helpless in the grave, grace carries us to the embrace of God.

—IN CHRIST'S IMAGE TRAINING

NOTES/SCRIPTURES/DATE

_____

_____

_____

_____

WORDS OF GRACE

Paul says that grace saved us "through faith." Faith unlocks the power of grace and releases it to function in our world – and faith itself is another gift of God. The difference between both gifts is that the grace–gift must be activated by the faith–gift. We must believe that God is "rich in mercy." We must accept as true that God loves us with "great love." We must not doubt He atoned for "our transgressions." We must be confident we are "alive together with Christ" (Eph. 2:4–5). Grace works through faith. Believing the words of grace unlocks the power of grace.

—In Christ's Image Training

NOTES/SCRIPTURES/DATE

_____

_____

_____

_____

LIKE A WATERED GARDEN

GOD'S PROMISE

True, grace is God's unmerited favor. Yet unmerited favor is only one aspect of grace. Grace is God's promise to do for us what we cannot do for ourselves. Consider Abraham. The Bible says he "believed God, and it was credited to him as righteousness" (Rom. 4:3). Abraham didn't just believe there was a God; he believed that what God promised would come to pass in his life. God promised to do for Abraham what Abraham and Sarah could not fulfill on their own. This is the glory of God's grace: it accomplishes for us what is otherwise impossible.

—IN CHRIST'S IMAGE TRAINING

NOTES/SCRIPTURES/DATE

_____

_____

_____

_____

SECURED IN GOD

The battle we face

is not one of action

but direction:

we must ascend vertically

to be successful horizontally.

A soul secured in God

secures victory in life.

—IN CHRIST'S IMAGE TRAINING

NOTES/SCRIPTURES/DATE

_____

_____

_____

_____

_____

THE WORD IS REALITY

God speaks in completed realities. In other words, when the Most High said, "Let there be light," it was not just sound that came out of His mouth, it was the actual substance of light. In the language of men and angels, words define reality, but in the language of God the Word is reality.

—IN CHRIST'S IMAGE TRAINING

NOTES/SCRIPTURES/DATE

_____
_____
_____
_____
_____

WHEN HE REMOVES

We should remember that when
the Lord removes our burdens,
He is also removing our excuses.

—In Christ's Image Training

NOTES/SCRIPTURES/DATE

_____

_____

_____

FILLED WITH JESUS

This is what revival and visitation
look like: people filled with
the presence and power of Jesus!

—The Days of His Presence

NOTES/SCRIPTURES/DATE

_____

_____

_____

OUR FAITH RESTORED

Most things we receive from God arrive via our asking, seeking and knocking. In the book of James, we find that we have not because we ask not. Consider: David was a man hunted by Saul and slandered throughout Israel – a man with many reasons to fear. Yet instead, he lived boldly. Where did David's confidence come from? He said, "I sought the Lord, and He answered me, and delivered me from all my fears" (Ps. 34:4). David wasn't delivered from fear simply in the routine of life's course. No, he said, "I sought the Lord ... and [He] delivered me." When we seek God, our faith is restored. As we draw near to God, our fears are subdued.

—I WILL BE FOUND BY YOU

NOTES/SCRIPTURES/DATE

_____

_____

_____

_____

PRAYER COVERS

True intercessory prayer is born of love and comes in the midst of sin and need. It comes not to condemn but to cover. All nations sin. All cultures have moral crises such as ours. Yet these times can become turning points if, in the time of our distress, God's people humble themselves. If we turn away from evil and pray, seeking the face and not just the hand of God, we will find the Most High will release His mercy on our land.

—THE POWER OF ONE CHRISTLIKE LIFE

NOTES/SCRIPTURES/DATE

_____

_____

_____

_____

_____

SEEING GOD AS HE IS

True worship is the consequence

of seeing God as He is.

It springs naturally from a soul

washed in Christ's blood,

then purified by God's love.

It rises like incense

from a heart without idols.

—HOLINESS, TRUTH AND THE PRESENCE OF GOD

NOTES/SCRIPTURES/DATE

_____

_____

_____

_____

_____

TO HELP OTHERS

Jesus paralleled speaking to people about their sins with taking a speck out of someone's eye. The eye is the most tender, most sensitive part of our body. How do you take a speck out of someone's eye? Very carefully! First, you must win their trust. This means consistently demonstrating an attitude that does not judge or instinctively condemn. To help others, Jesus tells us, we must first see clearly.

—THE THREE BATTLEGROUNDS

NOTES/SCRIPTURES/DATE

_____

_____

_____

_____

I FIND CHRIST

I have discovered that each time I seek God, the deliberate movement of my heart toward Him leads me to far more than just an answer to prayer. I actually find Christ, my Redeemer – the living One, the lover of my soul. I have an answer, but I also have an ally whose wisdom and incalculable power transforms all things with His Word.

—I WILL BE FOUND BY YOU

NOTES/SCRIPTURES/DATE

_____

_____

_____

_____

_____

CHRIST'S MERCY

As for us, until Christ opens the book and breaks the seals of wrath (Rev. 5), we must stand in intercession before God as ambassadors of the Lamb (2 Cor. 5:20). We are not minimizing sin when we maximize Christ's mercy. There is a difference between whitewashing sin and bloodwashing it.

—THE POWER OF ONE CHRISTLIKE LIFE

NOTES/SCRIPTURES/DATE

_____

_____

_____

_____

_____

SEPARATED UNTO

Holiness produces separation
from sin, but mere separation
from sin cannot produce holiness.
It is not the absence of sin
that produces our sanctification;
holiness comes from being separated
unto the living presence of God.
As He said, "You shall be holy,
for I am holy" (1 Pet. 1:16).

—HOLINESS, TRUTH AND THE PRESENCE OF GOD

NOTES/SCRIPTURES/DATE

_____

_____

_____

_____

PERSONAL REVIVAL

Some say it's too late for revival. I disagree. Maybe they do not have faith for a national revival, but as individuals we certainly can have a personal revival. Indeed, if we truly turn to God, awaiting us are "times of refreshing … from the presence of the Lord" (Acts 3:19). Additionally, a local church can turn to God and see a strong revival (2 Chron. 7:14). Furthermore, a city can also experience an outpouring of grace (Matt. 12:41). Don't tell me revival is not possible. Revival can begin right now, the moment we adamantly say "*Yes!*" to God.

—IN CHRIST'S IMAGE TRAINING

NOTES/SCRIPTURES/DATE

_____

_____

_____

AT HIS FEET

When I pray, I often begin

with this simple prayer:

Holy Spirit, lead me into

the presence of Jesus.

Lead me to where I hear His voice.

Guide me to where I am sitting

at His feet, where He can correct me

and, in His love, heal me.

—IN CHRIST'S IMAGE TRAINING

NOTES/SCRIPTURES/DATE

_____

_____

_____

_____

_____

WORSHIP

The "ship" that takes us safely
through the storms of life is worship.

—In Christ's Image Training

NOTES/SCRIPTURES/DATE

_____

_____

_____

IF WE ABIDE

Purity of heart can be reached
and maintained if we abide
in fellowship with God's Word.

—In Christ's Image Training

NOTES/SCRIPTURES/DATE

_____

_____

_____

YOU CAN, TOO

It was 1970. I was a new Christian but still very much a novice. Yet I was earnest, so when a church leader asked me to teach a small group at a nearby Bible college, I accepted. Still, I was nervous and my anxiety heightened when, as we drove to the study, the three others in the car warned me that the attenders would likely challenge every premise in my talk. Instantly my confidence deflated, and I began to quietly pray, "Lord, help! Give me a sign that I can do this." The closer we got, the more emphatically I prayed: "Lord, tell me I can do this!" Suddenly I noticed a hotel that we were passing: *The Franciscan*. However, the sign had a flaw. There was too much space between the "s" and the "c" so that, to me, it said "FRANCIS CAN." Amazing! I asked the Lord for a sign and He gave me an actual, large, glowing red neon sign! The truth is, if I can, you can, too.

—IN CHRIST'S IMAGE TRAINING

NOTES/SCRIPTURES/DATE

_____

_____

_____

TRUE REPENTANCE

In humility we not only

acknowledge our need,

we take full responsibility for it.

We offer no defense to God

for our fallen condition.

We've come not to explain ourselves

but to wash ourselves in

the blood of Christ and be changed.

—IN CHRIST'S IMAGE TRAINING

NOTES/SCRIPTURES/DATE

_____

_____

_____

_____

_____

LOVING DISCERNMENT

There are many who suppose
they are receiving
the Lord's discernment
concerning one thing or another.
Perhaps in some things they are;
only God knows.
But many are void of love
and simply judging others
and calling it discernment.

—SPIRITUAL DISCERNMENT AND THE MIND OF CHRIST

NOTES/SCRIPTURES/DATE

_____

_____

_____

_____

_____

PERFECT ENVIRONMENT

For all those outraged by the sinful conditions in our world, before you allow bitter anger to corrupt your soul, remember: We need an imperfect world if we will grow in Christ's likeness. We need actual enemies, for without them our love would never grow beyond its human boundaries. We need adversaries who want to destroy us, not just sparring partners who are actually on our side. You see, this sinful world is the perfect environment for God to fulfill His original purpose: man in the image of Christ.

—IN CHRIST'S IMAGE TRAINING

NOTES/SCRIPTURES/DATE

_____

_____

_____

_____

_____

FIRST HAVE PEACE

When the heart has unrest it cannot hear from God. Therefore, we must learn to mistrust our judgment when our heart is bitter, angry, ambitious or harboring strife for any reason. The Scriptures tell us to "let the peace of Christ rule [act as arbiter] in [our] hearts" (Col. 3:15). To hear consistently and clearly from God, we must first have peace.

—SPIRITUAL DISCERNMENT AND THE MIND OF CHRIST

NOTES/SCRIPTURES/DATE

_____

_____

_____

_____

_____

TWO THINGS ONLY

There are so many things to occupy our minds: so many books, so many examples, so many good teachings that deserve our attention, that say, "Here is a truth."

But as I have been serving the Lord these past years, He has led me to seek for two things and two things only: to know the heart of God in Christ and to know my own heart in Christ's light.

—HOLINESS, TRUTH AND THE PRESENCE OF GOD

NOTES/SCRIPTURES/DATE

_____

_____

_____

_____

GREAT LOVE

Just after Jesus speaks of mountain-moving faith, He says, "Whenever you stand praying, forgive, if you have anything against anyone" (Mark 11:23–25). Consider the nature of a heart that never holds unforgiveness toward anyone. This is a heart controlled by love. You see, Jesus connects the power of great faith with the motive of great love.

—In Christ's Image Training

NOTES/SCRIPTURES/DATE

_____

_____

_____

_____

NOT MY WILL BUT THINE

If we are continually

telling the Holy Spirit

where we want to go

we neutralize our capacity

to hear where

He wants to take us.

—IN CHRIST'S IMAGE TRAINING

NOTES/SCRIPTURES/DATE

_____

_____

_____

_____

_____

THE PERFECT SHELTER

Be specific about your flaws when you submit yourself to God. Do not rationalize your sins or blame others for your iniquity. The sacrifice of Christ is a perfect shelter of grace enabling all men to deal honestly with their sins. So be truthful with God. No condemnation awaits you. The Lord will not be shocked by your sins. He loved you without restraint even when sin was rampant within you; how much more will He continue to love you as you seek to be free from iniquity.

—THE THREE BATTLEGROUNDS

NOTES/SCRIPTURES/DATE

_____

_____

_____

_____

_____

HOW CHRISTLIKE

The true measure of spirituality

is not how angry

we become toward sinners

but how Christlike.

Our mission is not to see

evil men destroyed

but to see them redeemed.

—THE POWER OF ONE CHRISTLIKE LIFE

NOTES/SCRIPTURES/DATE

_____

_____

_____

_____

_____

REFLECTION

My wife and I once lived in an area where a beautiful red cardinal kept its nest. Cardinals are very territorial and will fight off intruding cardinals zealously. At that time, we owned a van that had large side mirrors and chrome bumpers. Occasionally, the cardinal would attack the bumpers or mirrors, thinking his reflection was another bird. One day, as I watched the cardinal assail the mirror, I thought, "What a foolish creature; his enemy is merely the reflection of himself." Immediately the Lord spoke to my heart, "And so also are many of your enemies the reflection of yourself." Before we have any strategy for attacking Satan, we must make sure that the real enemy is not our own carnal nature. We must ask ourselves, *"Are the things oppressing us today the harvest of what we planted yesterday?"*

—THE THREE BATTLEGROUNDS

NOTES/SCRIPTURES/DATE

_____

_____

_____

WAR ON GRUMBLING

Personally, I've declared war on grumbling. I've declared that an unthankful heart is an enemy to God's will. Can you join me with this? Can we crucify a murmuring spirit? We have received too much from God to allow ourselves opportunities for unbelief. We have received too many gifts and privileges to allow a grumbling, murmuring heart to disqualify us from our destiny.

—A HOUSE UNITED

NOTES/SCRIPTURES/DATE

_____

_____

_____

_____

STANDING

No one can truly stand against
the enemy if they are unsure
of their standing before God.

—THE POWER OF COVENANT PRAYER

NOTES/SCRIPTURES/DATE

_____

_____

_____

PRIDE IS MOST LETHAL

Of all sins, pride is the most lethal,
for it guards and protects
all our other vices.

—IN CHRIST'S IMAGE TRAINING

NOTES/SCRIPTURES/DATE

_____

_____

_____

HIS GRACE

Truth without grace

is only half true.

Grace without truth,

is an untruth.

Working together,

what God's truth demands,

His grace will provide.

—HOLINESS, TRUTH AND THE PRESENCE OF GOD

NOTES/SCRIPTURES/DATE

_____

_____

_____

_____

_____

REVEAL HIM

Our goal is not only to speak the truth but to actually communicate it. Christ wants us to reach people. Thus He calls us to go extra miles and to turn our cheek when struck. We are to genuinely love our enemies, not just try to correct them. You see, our truth is not just religious dogma; truth is a living person, the Lord Jesus Christ. And our goal is to actually reveal Him to the world around us.

—IN CHRIST'S IMAGE TRAINING

NOTES/SCRIPTURES/DATE

_____

_____

_____

_____

ALL WE HAVE

When the Lord fed the 5,000, He took the limited resources the disciples had – the five loaves and two fish – and He fed the multitudes (Matt. 14:13–21). The Lord has proven many times that we do not need to stockpile great resources before we attempt the impossible. As long as we remain in a blessable, surrendered state in the hands of the Master, our few loaves and fish are enough. What we have learned is that Jesus does not need a lot to work miracles; He just needs all we have.

—In Christ's Image Training

NOTES/SCRIPTURES/DATE

_____

_____

_____

_____

TENACITY

We should not interpret

divine delays as evidence

of divine reluctance.

Delays are tools God uses

to perfect and deepen our faith.

Christ is looking to develop tenacity

in us that prevails in spite of

delays and setbacks.

—THE POWER OF COVENANT PRAYER

NOTES/SCRIPTURES/DATE

_____

_____

_____

_____

BETA

When a new computer program is almost ready, the designers will release what is called a "beta" version. *Beta* means that the program is mostly working but still needs further testing under a variety of new conditions. It's my experience that most Christians are in beta: they are mostly working but still in the testing stage of their development. The Lord is looking to see how you handle discouragement or slander, fear or temptation. Once you pass this time of testing, you can be sure a greater release is coming.

—IN CHRIST'S IMAGE TRAINING

NOTES/SCRIPTURES/DATE

_____

_____

_____

_____

_____

IT TESTED HIM

A true word from God

will test you before it fulfills you.

Consider Joseph:

"Until the time

that his word came to pass,

the word of the Lord

tested him" (Ps. 105:19).

—IN CHRIST'S IMAGE TRAINING

NOTES/SCRIPTURES/DATE

_____

_____

_____

_____

_____

HUMBLE OURSELVES

Just as our love for God

is not complete until it manifests

as love for our neighbors,

so our humility toward God

finds maturity

when we can humble ourselves

to one another.

—IN CHRIST'S IMAGE TRAINING

NOTES/SCRIPTURES/DATE

_____

_____

_____

_____

CHRIST'S LOVE

There are two conditions of the heart no one can hide: one is when our heart is filled with love and the other when we are infected with bitterness. Either condition can take over our thoughts and both can filter our entire view of life. As followers of Jesus Christ, we must make our highest quest to possess hearts full of God's love. Indeed, how successful we are at revealing Christ's love is the true measure of our spirituality.

—IN CHRIST'S IMAGE TRAINING

NOTES/SCRIPTURES/DATE

_____

_____

_____

_____

_____

OUR GIANTS

Our journey into Christ is,
at the same time, His journey into us.
You see, we are His promised land.
We can be assured that the giants
in our lives, though
they may have humiliated us,
they will never humiliate Him.
He shall conquer each of our
enemies, even death,
and dwell in us forever.

—THE POWER OF ONE CHRISTLIKE LIFE

NOTES/SCRIPTURES/DATE

_____

_____

_____

HIS LIFE THROUGH US

Paul wrote,

"I have been crucified with Christ;

and it is no longer I who live,

but Christ lives in me" (Gal. 2:20).

God's goal is that, through

the Holy Spirit, Jesus Christ

would actually, functionally and

powerfully live His life through us.

—IN CHRIST'S IMAGE TRAINING

NOTES/SCRIPTURES/DATE

_____

_____

_____

_____

_____

OUR WALK WITH GOD

The confidence

we need

to face tomorrow

is rooted in

the quality of our walk

with God today.

—THE DAYS OF HIS PRESENCE

NOTES/SCRIPTURES/DATE

_____

_____

_____

_____

_____

CHOOSE LIGHT

You cannot serve two masters. You cannot serve light and darkness, sin and righteousness, self and God. Light is within us but so also is darkness. Our world is a world in darkness. Our ancestors were sons of darkness. Our carnal minds yet remain theaters of darkness. In a world of choices, we must choose light. If we would know the coming baptism of light, we must reject doublemindedness and the many seductions of darkness (Luke 11:34 KJV).

—HOLINESS, TRUTH AND THE PRESENCE OF GOD

NOTES/SCRIPTURES/DATE

_____

_____

_____

_____

_____

YOU ARE WITH ME

David wrote, "Even though I walk through the valley of the shadow of death, I fear no evil; for You are with me" (Ps. 23:4). There is a place of walking with God where we simply fear no evil. David faced a lion, a bear, and a giant. In this psalm he stood in the "shadow of death" itself, yet he had no dread of evil. David's trust was in the Lord. He said, "For You are with me." Because God is with you, every adversity you face will unfold in victory.

—THE THREE BATTLEGROUNDS

NOTES/SCRIPTURES/DATE

_____

_____

_____

_____

_____

"WAR MODE SWITCH"

Jesus was always aware that He lived in a war zone. No matter what He was doing – whether He was laughing with sinners or driving out demons, whether He was healing the sick or training followers – beneath the surface of His outer activities the "war mode switch" in Jesus' mind was always on.

—THIS DAY WE FIGHT!

NOTES/SCRIPTURES/DATE

_____

_____

_____

_____

_____

LET US PRESS IN

These are the "difficult times" Paul warns about (2 Tim. 3:1). Yes, our world is full of artificially sweetened, salt-free Christians who are trodden underfoot by men. We must not assume it cannot happen to us. Yet it is in this very environment that our Father has purposed to reveal Christ in us. Even now our destiny is courting our preparation. Let us, therefore, press toward full transformation!

—THE DAYS OF HIS PRESENCE

NOTES/SCRIPTURES/DATE

_____

_____

_____

_____

WE DISCOVER

The Bible tells us to
"Train up a child in the way
he should go, even when he is old
he will not depart from it"
(Prov. 22:6).
What we discover for ourselves
is that between "child" and "old"
God makes prayer warriors
of the parents.

—IN CHRIST'S IMAGE TRAINING

NOTES/SCRIPTURES/DATE

_____

_____

_____

_____

_____

STEADFAST PRAYER

Stay with your prayer. Don't back down. Even if you are hurt or disappointed by those you are praying for, or should you suffer painful delays, stay focused. If you maintain your faithfulness even though you are wounded, you will gain spiritual currency. Indeed, the steadfast prayer of the wounded intercessor holds great sway upon the heart of God.

—IN CHRIST'S IMAGE TRAINING

NOTES/SCRIPTURES/DATE

_____

_____

_____

_____

_____

PRESENT FULFILLMENT

The Lord's Prayer is Heaven's "Pledge of Allegiance." At its core, it is a faith-decree that God's will, through our living union with Christ, should be accomplished today on earth as it is in Heaven. Where is the room for compromise in those words? Yes, there will be an ultimate fulfillment at the return of Christ, but let us not miss the present fulfillment available now! For Jesus is saying that, with miraculous power, abounding joy and unwavering mercy, the will of God can be fulfilled in our world today as it is fulfilled in Heaven!

—IN CHRIST'S IMAGE TRAINING

NOTES/SCRIPTURES/DATE

_____

_____

_____

_____

FROM OUR HEARTS

Too often, as Christians,

we define ourselves by what

we do for God rather than what

we become to Him.

What pleases the Father most

is not what proceeds

from our hands

but what rises from our hearts.

—IN CHRIST'S IMAGE TRAINING

NOTES/SCRIPTURES/DATE

_____

_____

_____

_____

_____

TEST

When you pass a test from God,

three things occur:

you gain new spiritual power,

you experience the Lord's pleasure,

and then, after a short season,

you graduate into

something more difficult.

—IN CHRIST'S IMAGE TRAINING

NOTES/SCRIPTURES/DATE

_____

_____

_____

_____

CALLED TO POSSESS

Multitudes will sit in their easy chairs
and read about God's promises,
but you and I are called
not only to know God's promises
but to possess them
and walk them out.
You see, the real question for us
as Christians is not "Are you saved?"
but "Are you overcoming?"

—THIS DAY WE FIGHT!

NOTES/SCRIPTURES/DATE

_____

_____

_____

_____

_____

LIKE A WATERED GARDEN

THE PLEASURE OF GOD

Jesus not only asks the Father to forgive those who have wounded Him, but also numbers Himself with the transgressors and intercedes for them (Isa. 53:12). He does this because the Father takes "no pleasure in the death of the wicked" (Ezek. 33:11), and it is the pleasure of God that Jesus seeks.

—IN CHRIST'S IMAGE TRAINING

NOTES/SCRIPTURES/DATE

_____

_____

_____

_____

_____

REDEMPTIVE HEART

I have found, through many years in ministry, that often the flawed reality that initially angered me about my church or city, in this very place was where God desired I become Christlike. True, when I first see the need, typically, my flesh reacts with criticism. But if I repent of just finding fault – if I pray and submit myself to Christ's heart – I soon discover there are many ways for me to participate in redeeming this situation, all of which fuel my spiritual growth. Indeed, by approaching the area of need with Christ's redemptive heart, the "flawed reality" I initially criticized ultimately became the land of my anointing.

—IN CHRIST'S IMAGE TRAINING

NOTES/SCRIPTURES/DATE

_____

_____

_____

BE WISE, NOT FEARFUL

Among all the weapons that a terrorist might have, his primary weapon is the psychology of terror. By committing and publishing his atrocities, he seeks to awaken fear in his enemies. Fear is like witchcraft. It depletes one's strength and causes confusion. It blurs vision and paralyzes one's ability to fight at full strength. Jesus said there would be wars and rumors of wars. He warned, "See that you are not frightened" (Matt. 24:6). Today, let us examine ourselves. Though we live in fearful times, let us make certain we are not living in fear. Be wise, but not fearful.

—In Christ's Image Training

NOTES/SCRIPTURES/DATE

_____

_____

_____

_____

_____

PRAYING FOR THEM

Today America is overstocked
with angry Christians.
What can we do?
We must turn indignation
into intercession.
We must make our heartache
work for us, aligning ourselves
with Christ in the prayer
of redemption - actually praying
for those who persecute us.

—THE POWER OF ONE CHRISTLIKE LIFE

NOTES/SCRIPTURES/DATE

_____

_____

_____

DO OUR JOB

We moan, groan

and complain

that our politicians

are not doing their job,

but when we fail to pray

for them,

neither are we doing our job.

—THIS DAY WE FIGHT!

NOTES/SCRIPTURES/DATE

_____

_____

_____

_____

_____

GET TO WORK

Be strong and courageous
and get to work.
Don't be frightened
by the size of the task,
for the Lord my God is with you;
He will not forsake you.
He will see to it that everything
is finished correctly.
–1 CHRONICLES 28:20 TLB–

NOTES/SCRIPTURES/DATE

_____

_____

_____

_____

_____

THE WORD IS GOD

Read the Bible with an attitude
of willingness, faith and humility,
and even if you cannot
fully obey the Word,
keep it, holding it in your heart.
For the Word is God,
and as we keep it,
it will germinate in our hearts
until it fulfills itself within us.

—HOLINESS, TRUTH AND THE PRESENCE OF GOD

NOTES/SCRIPTURES/DATE

_____

_____

_____

_____

_____

THE MIND OF CHRIST

Our goal is not merely

to possess discernment

as an isolated grace

but to possess the character

and motives of Christ.

If we gain the mind of Christ,

our discernment in all its various

expressions will be effective.

—IN CHRIST'S IMAGE TRAINING

NOTES/SCRIPTURES/DATE

_____

_____

_____

_____

_____

NO OTHER PLAN

From the beginning, to make man

in the divine image has been

the unwavering purpose of God.

On a cosmic scale,

this is the master plan.

—THE POWER OF ONE CHRISTLIKE LIFE

NOTES/SCRIPTURES/DATE

_____

_____

_____

HONESTY

Humility, at its root, starts with honesty.

—IN CHRIST'S IMAGE TRAINING

NOTES/SCRIPTURES/DATE

_____

_____

_____

A SPIRITUAL DEFENSE

A particular strength

of humility is that it builds

a spiritual defense

around one's soul,

limiting strife

and many of life's irritations

from stealing one's peace.

—IN CHRIST'S IMAGE TRAINING

NOTES/SCRIPTURES/DATE

_____

_____

_____

_____

_____

WITHOUT LOVE

It is true that without knowledge we will perish, but knowledge without love is itself a state of perishing.

—WHEN THE MANY ARE ONE

NOTES/SCRIPTURES/DATE

_____

_____

_____

THE PATH WE ARE ON

If we are habitually grumbling or complaining, we should beware: the path we are on leads away from Christ.

—A HOUSE UNITED

NOTES/SCRIPTURES/DATE

_____

_____

_____

LIKE A WATERED GARDEN

LEADERS PRAY

Church history began with its leadership devoted to the Word of God and to prayer (Acts 2:42; 6:4). Every day the leaders gathered to pray and minister to the Lord. In this clarity of vision and simplicity of purpose – with the Lord Himself working with the disciples (Mark 16:20) – the church never had greater power to impact the world.

—THE POWER OF COVENANT PRAYER

NOTES/SCRIPTURES/DATE

_____

_____

_____

_____

SATAN WANTS TO RULE

Satan is primarily a religious spirit.
He does not want to destroy the world;
he wants to rule it and be worshipped.

—IN CHRIST'S IMAGE TRAINING

NOTES/SCRIPTURES/DATE

_____

_____

_____

ONLY GOD CAN GIVE

We genuinely can have
unoffendable hearts, but first
we must stop looking to receive
from people what only God can give.

—IN CHRIST'S IMAGE TRAINING

NOTES/SCRIPTURES/DATE

_____

_____

_____

CHRIST'S PLEASURE

Each time we choose to pray for other Christians rather than just criticize, we become an answer to Christ's prayer for our unity (John 17). Every time we forgive those who have hurt us, we increase Christ's pleasure. When we unite in love and fellowship with other born-again congregations across racial or denominational lines, we increase the bliss in our Father's heart.

—A House United

NOTES/SCRIPTURES/DATE

_____

_____

_____

_____

_____

ONENESS

If we set our hearts to truly obey the Lord, we will ultimately find ourselves in a state of oneness with Him. Our oneness with God will facilitate oneness with our loved ones. Finally, if we remain faithful to God's will, His love in us will create a state of oneness with others in the body of Christ (John 17). Do we see this? If we can agree collectively to fully do God's will, it will lead to oneness with all whom we love. This state of deep spiritual fulfillment is called Heaven.

—IN CHRIST'S IMAGE TRAINING

NOTES/SCRIPTURES/DATE

_____

_____

_____

_____

CARRY THE CROSS

I have known some who were angry that an injustice was committed against them, even lamenting that the injustice they experienced was their cross. But, as I see it, they weren't carrying a cross – they were carrying a grudge. Indeed, we aren't carrying the cross of Christ until we forgive those who put us there.

—IN CHRIST'S IMAGE TRAINING

NOTES/SCRIPTURES/DATE

_____

_____

_____

_____

A HYPOCRITE IS...

It is vital we understand
that Jesus did not
condemn sinners;
He condemned hypocrites.
A hypocrite is a person
who excuses his own sin
while condemning
the sins of another.

—HOLINESS, TRUTH AND THE PRESENCE OF GOD

NOTES/SCRIPTURES/DATE

_____

_____

_____

_____

_____

AS LONG AS IT TAKES

The prophet Daniel prayed three times a day, every day, since his earliest years. He continued in prayer for nearly seventy years, until the time Jeremiah's prophecy came to pass! Yes, there are times when God acts quickly. More often, however, the work of God will take time. How long should we pray? We pray as long as it takes.

—THE POWER OF COVENANT PRAYER

NOTES/SCRIPTURES/DATE

_____

_____

_____

_____

_____

A TRUE FOUNDATION

If you truly seek to crucify your instinct to judge and genuinely are pursuing Christ's redemptive heart, you will have laid a true foundation for the gift of discernment. You will have prepared your heart to receive dreams, visions and insights from God. You will be unstained by human bias. You will possess the mind and heart of Christ.

—Spiritual Discernment and the Mind of Christ

NOTES/SCRIPTURES/DATE

_____

_____

_____

_____

_____

NATIONS WILL COME

"Arise, shine; for your light has come,
And the glory of the Lord
has risen upon you.
For behold, darkness
will cover the earth
And deep darkness the peoples;
But the Lord will rise upon you
And His glory will appear upon you.
Nations will come to your light,
And kings to the
brightness of your rising."
–Isaiah 60:1-3–

NOTES/SCRIPTURES/DATE

_____

_____

_____

STUDY HIS HEART

John tells us that the Law
came through Moses
but "grace and truth
were realized through Jesus Christ"
(John 1:17). Let us, therefore,
study the heart of Christ,
for if we would truly represent Him,
we too must speak
with both grace and truth.

—IN CHRIST'S IMAGE TRAINING

NOTES/SCRIPTURES/DATE

_____

_____

_____

_____

_____

THE SUBSTRUCTURE

In our desire to know God, we must discern this about the Almighty: He resists the proud, but His grace is drawn to the humble. Humility brings grace to our need, and grace alone can change our hearts. Humility, therefore, is the substructure of transformation. It is the escort of all virtues.

—HOLINESS, TRUTH AND THE PRESENCE OF GOD

NOTES/SCRIPTURES/DATE

_____

_____

_____

_____

HEARTS FULL OF LOVE

Jesus warned that, at the end of the age, iniquity would abound. As a result, the love of many would "grow cold" (Matt. 24:12). Yet He also said that simultaneously another reality will emerge in the end times: the Kingdom of Heaven, and it would be proclaimed in word and power as a witness to all nations (Matt. 24:14). What we must decide is which group we are in: those whose hearts are full of the offenses of man or those whose hearts are full of the love of God and neighbor, a people pressing into God's kingdom (Mark 12:28–33).

—In Christ's Image Training

NOTES/SCRIPTURES/DATE

_____

_____

_____

BECOME TRUE

Being false is natural to
the human heart; it is with humility
and effort that we become true.

—HOLINESS, TRUTH AND THE PRESENCE OF GOD

NOTES/SCRIPTURES/DATE

_____

_____

_____

WHEN THE STORM COMES

Jesus did not say "if" a storm arises, or "if" by chance the rain should fall – He says *when* the storm comes, *when* the rains fall. Everyone in this world will face storms at certain times of their lives.

—IN CHRIST'S IMAGE TRAINING

NOTES/SCRIPTURES/DATE

_____

_____

_____

RETURN TO LOVE

For those who say they have lost faith for America (or their nation), my response is that you didn't lose faith, you lost love. You were praying for revival, but instead evil increased and your heart hardened. Let me suggest that you forgive America and ask God to forgive and change your leaders as well. Return to love and you will return to faith, for "faith works through love" (Gal. 5:6) and "love believes all things" (1 Cor. 13:4–7). You see, you didn't lose faith, you lost love.

—IN CHRIST'S IMAGE TRAINING

NOTES/SCRIPTURES/DATE

_____

_____

_____

_____

JESUS IS A CRUTCH

When unbelievers tell me
that Jesus is a crutch,
I tell them they are right.
They just don't know
how lame they are.
Yes, Jesus is a crutch.
He's also legs to walk and
feet to dance.

—IN CHRIST'S IMAGE TRAINING

NOTES/SCRIPTURES/DATE

_____

_____

_____

_____

_____

BELIEVE HIS PROMISES

There will always be those
who openly doubt your faith.
They challenge,
"What if what you believe
doesn't come to pass?"
Listen, it's not my job
to fulfill God's promises.
My task is to believe them.

—IN CHRIST'S IMAGE TRAINING

NOTES/SCRIPTURES/DATE

_____

_____

_____

_____

_____

STOP FRETTING

If you have prayed through

and truly placed your burden

in the hands of God,

then stop fretting about it.

God calls us to be

prayer warriors,

not prayer worriers.

—IN CHRIST'S IMAGE TRAINING

NOTES/SCRIPTURES/DATE

_____

_____

_____

_____

_____

COMPELLED BY LOVE

The fact is, we are in a spiritual war and if we will succeed in these difficult days it will be, in part, because we have renounced the seductive limitations of a peacetime mentality. Indeed, we must embrace an aspect of spirituality that is unfamiliar to many Christians – one that is both militant and vigilant toward evil, yet compelled by the purity and fire of Christ's love.

—This Day We Fight!

NOTES/SCRIPTURES/DATE

_____

_____

_____

_____

_____

HEAVEN ADVANCES

The good news is that hell would not
be in such a frenzy if Heaven
were not advancing (Rev. 12:12).

—This Day We Fight!

NOTES/SCRIPTURES/DATE

_____

_____

_____

ARE WE READY?

When we entreat the Almighty
for His kingdom,
are we ready to surrender ours?.

—The Days of His Presence

NOTES/SCRIPTURES/DATE

_____

_____

_____

THE CHURCH PRAYS

Paul not only asked for prayer for boldness in speaking God's Word but also for protection as he faced "many adversaries" (1 Cor. 16:9). While we are learning to pray for secular leaders, perhaps we are failing to pray for our spiritual leaders. We assume they know how to protect themselves, yet recall that after James was killed by Herod, Peter was put in jail to suffer a similar fate (Acts 12). This time, however, "prayer for [Peter] was being made fervently by the church" (Acts 12:5). As a result, not only was Peter delivered, but Herod was struck by an angel and died. You see, there are some breakthroughs and certain levels of protection that only come because the church prays for its spiritual leaders.

—IN CHRIST'S IMAGE TRAINING

NOTES/SCRIPTURES/DATE

_____

_____

_____

THE LORD IS MY LIGHT

Do not rejoice over me, O my enemy.
Though I fall I will rise;
Though I dwell in darkness,
the Lord is a light for me.
–MICAH 7:8–

NOTES/SCRIPTURES/DATE

_____

_____

_____

SURRENDER SORROWS

The heart that surrenders
its sorrows to God,
surrenders its wounds to healing.

—I WILL BE FOUND BY YOU

NOTES/SCRIPTURES/DATE

_____

_____

_____

COMPROMISE WITH SIN

How a little leaven leavens the whole lump! A relatively minor sin that we do not attend to can lead to a major sin that destroys our lives. Judas "became a traitor." He started out in ministry loyal to Jesus, but then began lying about the finances until his deceitful exterior completely masked his ever darkening heart. Judas was a thief who became a traitor, eventually taking his own life. His compromise with sin destroyed him.

—THE POWER OF ONE CHRISTLIKE LIFE

NOTES/SCRIPTURES/DATE

_____

_____

_____

_____

SIN

Sin carries its own punishment.

—IN CHRIST'S IMAGE TRAINING

NOTES/SCRIPTURES/DATE

_____

_____

_____

FAITHFULLY OBEY

It is an indisputable truth:

the only way to prepare

for Jesus' second coming

is to faithfully obey what

He commanded in His first coming.

—IN CHRIST'S IMAGE TRAINING

NOTES/SCRIPTURES/DATE

_____

_____

_____

NOT JUST CRITICS

In contrast to those who only find fault, the Lord is raising up true Christ-followers. When they see a need in their church or community or nation, instead of just criticizing, they go "into the breaches" and stand in the gap (Ezek. 13:3–5). They are not simply critics; they are Heaven-sent agents of redemption.

—THE THREE BATTLEGROUNDS

NOTES/SCRIPTURES/DATE

THE LIVING FLAME

The devil knows

you are a Christian,

not just because he heard you

say a sinner's prayer,

but because, when you prayed,

he saw the living flame of

Christ Himself enter your heart.

—In Christ's Image Training

NOTES/SCRIPTURES/DATE

_____

_____

_____

_____

_____

SINS BECOME LIGHT

Paul wrote, "We have renounced the things hidden because of shame" (2 Cor. 4:2). When we expose and confess our sins, they no longer are in darkness (secrecy). Indeed, when a light is turned on in a dark room, the darkness becomes light. So also when we bring our sins out of darkness and expose them to light, they vanish in the brightness of God's forgiveness; they become light.

—HOLINESS, TRUTH AND THE PRESENCE OF GOD

NOTES/SCRIPTURES/DATE

_____

_____

_____

_____

HE CARES

Yes, the Lord cares even for the little things that are in our lives. He cares because we care. Thus, He tells us to cast all our cares upon Him. Yet, to be true, He is more concerned with our full conversion than our fleshly comfort; He seeks to establish in us true holiness rather than false happiness.

—IN CHRIST'S IMAGE TRAINING

NOTES/SCRIPTURES/DATE

_____

_____

_____

_____

_____

BAPTISM OF LIGHT

To become overly focused on the details of the end of the age is like standing before a glorious sunrise yet becoming distracted by the shadows it causes.

Therefore, let us not become so absorbed with the dark movement of end-time shadows that we lose focus on Christ, whose day is simultaneously dawning upon us. Many have written about the shadows; my goal is to help prepare God's people for the coming baptism of light.

—THE DAYS OF HIS PRESENCE

NOTES/SCRIPTURES/DATE

_____

_____

_____

EXPECTATIONS

No matter how true a dream or vision from God may be, almost without exception it will not be fulfilled as we imagine. All our expectations are, at best, daydreams. In my years of ministry, I have had many promises from God fulfilled. However, never once did He fulfill His word precisely as I imagined. God's will is full of surprises. His promise will always come forth "exceedingly abundantly above all that we ask or think" (Eph. 3:20 NKJV).

—IN CHRIST'S IMAGE TRAINING

NOTES/SCRIPTURES/DATE

_____

_____

_____

_____

LOVELESS HEART

Six times in Matthew 24 Jesus warned of rampant deception at the end of the age. Certainly, false prophets and false teachers are among us, and they are misleading many. Yes, we must zealously guard our doctrines, and with passion pursue the truth. Yet for all the heresy in our world one form of deception goes almost unchecked in the church: the apostasy of a loveless heart. What value is it to possess right doctrines if our love for others has grown cold?

—IN CHRIST'S IMAGE TRAINING

NOTES/SCRIPTURES/DATE

_____

_____

_____

_____

THE NEW MANTLE

Here is what I have discovered: just before the Lord releases a new mantle or anointing upon an individual, He will often "dis-mantle" that individual's previous level of service. This dismantling may not feel good. We may pass through a season of brokenness. But if we keep faith during the process, the new mantle will come. When it does, you will have greater conformity to Christ and, thus, greater power.

—IN CHRIST'S IMAGE TRAINING

NOTES/SCRIPTURES/DATE

_____

_____

_____

_____

LISTEN, OBEY

What I'm saying is this: we need to cultivate a listening ear and an obedient heart. Not only are there miracles awaiting us, there are people the Lord needs us to encourage (Isa. 50:4). So today take time to wait and listen to the Holy Spirit, then purpose to obey what you sense He is telling you. See what kind of day you have.

—IN CHRIST'S IMAGE TRAINING

NOTES/SCRIPTURES/DATE

_____

_____

_____

_____

_____

WHAT WE REALLY NEED

I was speaking at a conference on the power of the cross and the need for self-denial. Afterwards a pastor approached. He was concerned, saying my teaching about dying to self sounded like an Eastern religion. I asked him if he knew that Christianity didn't originate in America, that it actually is a Middle Eastern religion? You see, we in the West think Christianity is about self-gratification, but what we really need is self-denial so that the love of Christ can rule in our hearts.

—IN CHRIST'S IMAGE TRAINING

NOTES/SCRIPTURES/DATE

_____

_____

_____

_____

_____

THE UNFOLDING

This reality that we call Christianity,
in the beginning
looks a little like a religion with
a new set of rules.
Yet if we will stay with it,
we will discover that Christianity
is not just a moral upgrade.
It is, in truth, the unfolding
of God's glory in man.

—IN CHRIST'S IMAGE TRAINING

NOTES/SCRIPTURES/DATE

_____

_____

_____

_____

_____

THEY WILL STILL BEAR FRUIT

Planted in the house of the Lord,

[The righteous] thrive

in the courtyards of our God.

They will still bear fruit in old age,

healthy and green,

To declare: "The Lord is just;

He is my rock, and there is

no unrighteousness in Him."

−Psalm 92:13–15 hcsb−

NOTES/SCRIPTURES/DATE

_____

_____

_____

_____

ABOUNDING LOVE

Paul wrote, "And this I pray,

that your love may abound

still more and more

in real knowledge and all discernment"

(Phil. 1:9).

True discernment comes from

abounding love.

What is abounding love? It is love that

leaps out from us toward others.

—THE THREE BATTLEGROUNDS

NOTES/SCRIPTURES/DATE

_____

_____

_____

_____

_____

GOD'S GLORY

The vision of Christ's glory manifest through us strikes some as heresy. Yet isn't this unfolding manifestation of Christ in us the focus of Paul in 2 Corinthians 3? He wrote, "But we all, with unveiled face, beholding as in a mirror the glory of the Lord, are being transformed into the same image from glory to glory" (v. 18). Didn't Paul use Moses as an example of one whose face shone with the reflected glory of God (v. 7)? Perhaps we have lived for so long in churches where the glory has departed that we think the return of God's glory is heresy.

—THE DAYS OF HIS PRESENCE

NOTES/SCRIPTURES/DATE

_____

_____

_____

_____

_____

NOT HARNESSED

Should the lowliness of our sinful state have veto power over the enormity of God's promises? May it never be! For Scripture assures us that our call, even as lowly as we feel at times, is an upward climb that relies upon faith in God's abilities and trust in our Lord's redemption. We are not harnessed to our flaws and weaknesses. Rather in Spirit-to-spirit fusion we are united to the resurrection power of Christ! Our call is not merely to attend church but to walk with God, the Almighty One who has predestined us to be "conformed to the image of His Son" (Rom. 8:29).

—SPIRITUAL DISCERNMENT AND THE MIND OF CHRIST

NOTES/SCRIPTURES/DATE

_____

_____

_____

THE NATURE OF JESUS

Victory begins with the name of Jesus on our lips, but it is not consummated until the nature of Jesus is in our hearts.

—THE THREE BATTLEGROUNDS

NOTES/SCRIPTURES/DATE

_____

_____

_____

THE FULLNESS OF CHRIST

We are called to attain "the measure of the stature which belongs to the fullness of Christ" (Eph. 4:13).

—IN CHRIST'S IMAGE TRAINING

NOTES/SCRIPTURES/DATE

_____

_____

_____

DISCERNMENT

Picture, if you will, a long-haired young man. He is unkempt; tattoos are on his arms. It is night and he is walking toward you on a lonely street. It is easy to judge this man after the obvious. Now look at him in the same setting but as his mother. You can still see his outer appearance but you also have insight into his life and hope for his future. You see a little boy growing up fatherless, a child without friends. Your commitment is deep toward him having been sustained by love since his birth. You see, false discernment sees the outside of a person and assumes it knows the inside. True discernment is empowered by love.

—SPIRITUAL DISCERNMENT AND THE MIND OF CHRIST

NOTES/SCRIPTURES/DATE

_____

_____

_____

TRANSPARENCY

No confessing sinner was ever isolated from the Messiah's grace; no sin or flaw rendered one exiled from God's mercy. Only one type of person consistently found himself outside Christ's transforming power: the hypocrite. A hypocrite is a master of disguises. Thus Jesus elevates the transparent heart of the little child as being "greatest in the kingdom of Heaven."

—HOLINESS, TRUTH AND THE PRESENCE OF GOD

NOTES/SCRIPTURES/DATE

_____

_____

_____

_____

A CHRISTIAN

A Christian is not just a person going
to Heaven. Shouldn't a Christian also be
a person coming from Heaven, with
the goods, power and virtue of Heaven?

—SPIRITUAL DISCERNMENT AND THE MIND OF CHRIST

NOTES/SCRIPTURES/DATE

_____

_____

_____

IT IS THE SONG

Thanksgiving is the song of faith.

—IN CHRIST'S IMAGE TRAINING

NOTES/SCRIPTURES/DATE

_____

_____

_____

NUMBERED WITH US

This is our Lord and Redeemer, the Great High Priest who, in eternal intercession, numbered Himself with us sinners (Isa. 53). When we are born again, we receive Him not as a mere doctrine but as the living One who works to conform us to Himself (Rom. 8:29). As He numbered Himself with us, so we also identify with those we pray for, whether they are our friends or enemies. As He said, "As the Father has sent Me, I also send you" (John 20:21).

—IN CHRIST'S IMAGE TRAINING

NOTES/SCRIPTURES/DATE

_____

_____

_____

_____

_____

LIKE THE SPRING RAIN

"Come, let us return to the Lord.

For He has torn us, but He will heal us;

He has wounded us, but He will bandage us.

He will revive us after two days;

He will raise us up on the third day,

That we may live before Him.

So let us know,

let us press on to know the Lord.

His going forth is as certain as the dawn;

And He will come to us like the rain,

Like the spring rain watering the earth."

–Hosea 6:1-3–

NOTES/SCRIPTURES/DATE

_____

_____

_____

HUMILITY

In the kingdom, there are no great men of God, just humble men whom God has chosen to use greatly. How do we know when we are humble? When God speaks, we tremble. God is looking for a man who trembles at His words. Such a man will find the Spirit of God resting upon him; he will become a dwelling place for the Almighty.

—HOLINESS, TRUTH AND THE PRESENCE OF GOD

NOTES/SCRIPTURES/DATE

_____

_____

_____

_____

UNCHANGED

QUESTION: What will happen if you stop seeking God and turn spiritually lukewarm?

THE ANSWER IS, probably nothing will happen. Meteors won't fall from Heaven onto your house. Life will continue pretty much as it was and nothing uncommon to all men will occur if you stop seeking God. You will remain as you have always been: unchanged. An unchanged life is judgment enough.

—IN CHRIST'S IMAGE TRAINING

NOTES/SCRIPTURES/DATE

_____

_____

_____

_____

_____

AMEN — SO BE IT

Perhaps we do not realize it but every time we say "Amen" to something, we are not just giving an emotional assent to what was said. *Amen* means more than "I agree." It also means, "So be it." In other words, don't just talk about the truth, be it. Don't just tell us the standard, attain it. Let's not just enjoy the teaching, let's live it. Let's not limit our Christianity to doctrines, let's actually become sons and daughters of the living God.

—IN CHRIST'S IMAGE TRAINING

NOTES/SCRIPTURES/DATE

_____

_____

_____

_____

_____

MAKE ROOM

What if the Holy Spirit actually desired to manifest Himself during our worship service? Would the Lord have to wait until we finished our scheduled programs? I respect and recognize the need for order; we need times for announcements and the predefined purposes that currently occupy Sunday mornings – these things are legitimate. But have we made room for God Himself?

—IN CHRIST'S IMAGE TRAINING

NOTES/SCRIPTURES/DATE

_____

_____

_____

_____

_____

NOT JUST NUMBERS

In the American church, we measure our success by the number of people who attend our church – and, yes, those numbers are important. Yet even more important than a packed church is the depth of Christ-centered unity between attending Christians. In the kingdom, as in poker, four of a kind beats a full house.

—IN CHRIST'S IMAGE TRAINING

NOTES/SCRIPTURES/DATE

_____

_____

_____

_____

_____

DO YOU KNOW?

The world is watching how we relate to those who are morally wrong, even when we are biblically right. And they are watching to see if we sound like the Savior or like the Pharisees.

Yet there is one thing more crucial than how the world sees us, and that is how Christ sees us. He is watching what is happening to our hearts. He asks each of us a simple question: Do you know what you're becoming?

—THE POWER OF ONE CHRISTLIKE LIFE

NOTES/SCRIPTURES/DATE

_____

_____

_____

_____

_____

JOB SECURITY

An imperfect world is job security
for an intercessor.

—IN CHRIST'S IMAGE TRAINING

NOTES/SCRIPTURES/DATE

_____

_____

_____

IT'S THE MAN

Remember, the way into the future
is not a plan,
it's the Man: Christ Jesus!

—IN CHRIST'S IMAGE TRAINING

NOTES/SCRIPTURES/DATE

_____

_____

_____

UNVEILING OF CHRIST

We have instructed the church in nearly everything except how to carry the presence of Christ. We have given people doctrines instead of deity; we've provided manuals instead of Emmanuel. What the church most desperately needs in this hour is the unveiling of Christ in His body. From today on, let our goal be this: to see the actual "life of Jesus ... manifested in our mortal flesh" (2 Cor. 4:11).

—In Christ's Image Training

NOTES/SCRIPTURES/DATE

_____

_____

_____

_____

_____

LIKE A WATERED GARDEN

OUR TRANSFORMATION

We should repent of carrying
the image of a Savior
who fails to confront our sin
or challenge our unbelief,
for such is a false image of God.
If we are to genuinely know Him,
we must accept this truth:
Jesus Christ is irrevocably committed
to our complete transformation!

—THE SHELTER OF THE MOST HIGH

NOTES/SCRIPTURES/DATE

_____

_____

_____

_____

_____

PRAY, NOT PREY

Jesus said the Father's house

would be called a house of prayer

for all nations.

Beloved, the Lord's house

is a holy place

where mercy streams from Heaven

to meet the needs of earth.

It is a place where we pray

for each other

rather than prey on each other.

—WHEN THE MANY ARE ONE

NOTES/SCRIPTURES/DATE

_____

_____

_____

_____

BE STILL, AND KNOW

Be still, and know that I am God;
I will be exalted among the nations,
I will be exalted in the earth.
–Psalm 46:10 niv–

NOTES/SCRIPTURES/DATE

_____

_____

_____

REPLICATION

The goal of true mentoring is
not blessing, but
replication of anointing.

—In Christ's Image Training

NOTES/SCRIPTURES/DATE

_____

_____

_____

HIS VERY NATURE

Christ and His Word are inseparable.
Jesus was not a man who became
the Word but the eternal Word
who became a man.
His very core nature is the
Word of God. And to reject or
ignore what He says is to reject or
ignore who He is.

—IN CHRIST'S IMAGE TRAINING

NOTES/SCRIPTURES/DATE

_____

_____

_____

_____

222

SPIRIT-LED

Do not accept that God has permanently hidden Himself from you, though during your trial it may seem so. We are learning to see in the dark and to hear in the silence. He is making Himself known to our inner man so we can be Spirit-led in spite of outer circumstances.

—IN CHRIST'S IMAGE TRAINING

NOTES/SCRIPTURES/DATE

_____

_____

_____

_____

_____

POWER TO DO

The proof that we have
truly received Christ's anointing
is that we have power,
at least in some measurable way,
to do what Jesus did.

—In Christ's Image Training

NOTES/SCRIPTURES/DATE

_____

_____

_____

VIRTUE

Virtue is its own reward.

—In Christ's Image Training

NOTES/SCRIPTURES/DATE

_____

_____

_____

OUR ATTITUDE

The very quality of one's life, whether we love it or hate it, is based upon how thankful we are toward God. Our attitude determines whether life is to us a place of blessedness or wretchedness. Indeed, looking at the same rose bush, some complain that roses have thorns while others rejoice that some thorns come with roses!

—THE SHELTER OF THE MOST HIGH

NOTES/SCRIPTURES/DATE

_____

_____

_____

_____

_____

THE FUTURE

The Lord does not

want us worrying

about the future;

He wants us to create it

through the knowledge

of His will

and the proclamation

of His Word.

—THIS DAY WE FIGHT!

NOTES/SCRIPTURES/DATE

_____

_____

_____

_____

GOD-ASSURED

Peace is the fruit of

being confident in God's love;

it is born of the revelation that,

regardless of the battle,

"greater is He who is in you than he

who is in the world" (1 John 4:4).

You are not self-assured,

you are God-assured.

—THE THREE BATTLEGROUNDS

NOTES/SCRIPTURES/DATE

_____

_____

_____

_____

_____

YOUR VISION

If you stumble, get up.

If you sin, repent. Whatever you do,

in spite of your feelings,

do not lose your vision

of attaining Christ's likeness.

Your spiritual vision is more important

than your physical vision. Without vision

you will perish (Prov. 29:18 KJV).

—HOLINESS, TRUTH AND THE PRESENCE OF GOD

NOTES/SCRIPTURES/DATE

_____

_____

_____

_____

_____

VIRTUE

The virtue of any institution

is not so much in its

doctrines or organization;

rather, its virtue resides

in the quality of person

it produces.

—WHEN THE MANY ARE ONE

NOTES/SCRIPTURES/DATE

_____

_____

_____

_____

_____

DO LIKEWISE

Many years ago I was part of a church group that, in spite of its good points, also had serious problems. At that time I was pastoring a small church and felt we should leave the parent organization because of its flaws. So my church and I began to prayerfully seek God for His will. After 40 days, I held my list of complaints before the Lord and prayed, "Lord, look at the errors in these people. Direct us, Lord. Should we leave or stay?" Immediately, speaking to my heart, the Lord replied, "Have you seen these things?" "Yes, Lord," I answered, "I have seen their sins." To which He said, "So also have I, but I died for them. You go and do likewise."

—THE THREE BATTLEGROUNDS

NOTES/SCRIPTURES/DATE

_____

_____

_____

FEAR OR FAITH

Scripture says that the sight of a figure walking on the water, coming toward them in the howling wind and darkness, turned the disciples' fear into terror. They cried out, "It is a ghost!" (Matt. 14:26). Note: Some of the things we label as "ghostly" or demonic, that terrify us in the middle of the night, are really the Lord setting the stage for a lesson on faith.

—THIS DAY WE FIGHT!

NOTES/SCRIPTURES/DATE

_____

_____

_____

_____

_____

BELIEVE GOD

The Bible says that Jesus is the "author and perfecter" of our faith (Heb. 12:2). Get used to the idea that the Son of God is seeking not only to inspire faith but to actually perfect it. Plan on the fact that, sooner or later, the real Jesus will require you to look the impossible straight in the eye and, without fear, believe God for miracles.

—IN CHRIST'S IMAGE TRAINING

NOTES/SCRIPTURES/DATE

_____

_____

_____

_____

_____

FORGIVING OFFENSES

Jesus tells us we must forgive

those who sin against us.

Indeed, the offenses

we do not forgive and transfer

to God in prayer

inevitably decay and become

a venom we transfer to others

through gossip.

—A HOUSE UNITED

NOTES/SCRIPTURES/DATE

_____

_____

_____

_____

_____

A PASSAGE

As we mature spiritually, in unfolding ways we realize that it is not "Christianity" living in us, it is Christ Himself. His Word speaks to our inner man, training, reproving and guiding us. The cross emerges off the printed page and stands before us, confronting us with our own Gethsemanes, our own Golgothas. We die to self, yet we live; yet it is not us who live, but Christ lives within us (Gal. 2:20). The cross that put my old nature to death now becomes a passage to resurrection life in the presence of God.

—HOLINESS, TRUTH AND THE PRESENCE OF GOD

NOTES/SCRIPTURES/DATE

_____

_____

_____

_____

_____

SUCH IS THE LIFE

Hypocrites love to judge;
it makes them feel superior.
But it shall not be so with you.
You must seek earnestly
for lowliness of heart.
Many zealous but proud Christians
fail to reach holiness because
they presume they are called
to judge others.

—HOLINESS, TRUTH AND THE PRESENCE OF GOD

NOTES/SCRIPTURES/DATE

_____

_____

_____

_____

_____

ALL FOR A SINNER

Anyone can judge, but can they save? Can they lay down their lives in love, intercession and faith for a sinner? Rather than just criticizing, can they fast and pray, asking God to supply the very virtue they deem is lacking? And then, can they persevere in love-motivated prayer until that fallen soul blooms in godliness? Such is the life Christ commands we follow!

—HOLINESS, TRUTH AND THE PRESENCE OF GOD

NOTES/SCRIPTURES/DATE

_____

_____

_____

_____

_____

THE BODY – UNITED

At some point between now and when Christ returns, leaders in the born-again church will begin to see division between their churches as sin against Christ. Congregations from different backgrounds will help one another when needs arise; pastors will pray with each other regularly, and Christians will be known for their love. The body of Christ will unite around Jesus and in their unity Christ Himself will be revealed. The bride will have made herself ready.

—IN CHRIST'S IMAGE TRAINING

NOTES/SCRIPTURES/DATE

_____

_____

_____

_____

TRUTH IS...

Men everywhere presume they know the "truth," but they have neither holiness nor power in their lives. Truth must be more than a museum of religious artifacts – mementos from when God once moved. Truth is knowing God's heart as it was revealed in Christ, and it is knowing our own hearts in the light of God's grace.

—HOLINESS, TRUTH AND THE PRESENCE OF GOD

NOTES/SCRIPTURES/DATE

_____

_____

_____

_____

_____

NO SUGGESTIONS

Christ has provided many things
for us, but one thing
He didn't give us was suggestions.

—IN CHRIST'S IMAGE TRAINING

NOTES/SCRIPTURES/DATE

_____

_____

_____

SELF-PITY

As pride protects
our other vices, so self-pity
keeps our wounds alive.

—IN CHRIST'S IMAGE TRAINING

NOTES/SCRIPTURES/DATE

_____

_____

_____

LAWS OF GOD

After seven years of madness, King Nebuchadnezzar acknowledged the absolute sovereignty of the Most High God (Dan. 4). Some may question the story of Nebuchadnezzar's insanity, but to them I say it is madness to think man can create a good, prosperous and safe society and, at the same time, reject the laws of God. Indeed, the nation that turns from God turns to madness and the breakdown of its culture.

—IN CHRIST'S IMAGE TRAINING

NOTES/SCRIPTURES/DATE

_____

_____

_____

_____

PEACE IS PROOF

Jesus gave His followers "author-ity over all the power of the enemy." And in the exercise of that authority, He assures us, "Nothing will injure you" (Luke 10:19 NLT). When you truly have authority over something, you can look at that adversary without worry, fear or anxiety. Your peace is the proof of your victory.

—IN CHRIST'S IMAGE TRAINING

NOTES/SCRIPTURES/DATE

_____

_____

_____

_____

AM I WALKING IN THIS?

A few years ago I added a new discipline to my study of God's Word. Instead of reading through the whole Bible, as was my custom, I focused only on the words of Jesus, approaching each promise or command deliberately, prayerfully, not rushing to fulfill a daily quota of so many chapters. I saw each verse as an aspect of the Lord's heart that I wanted to possess. This was an "inspection time" to see how truly I was walking as a disciple. So as I studied each verse, without defending or excusing myself, I asked, "Lord, am I walking in this? If not, what still do I lack?" You see, the goal is not just to know the truth of God, but to walk in it with a whole heart.

—IN CHRIST'S IMAGE TRAINING

NOTES/SCRIPTURES/DATE

_____

_____

_____

CANCEL YOUR PLANS

The psalmist said
"goodness and mercy
shall follow me all the days
of my life" (Ps. 23:6 NKJV).
Goodness and mercy,
not fear and depression.
I say it's time to cancel your plans
to be miserable.

—IN CHRIST'S IMAGE TRAINING

NOTES/SCRIPTURES/DATE

_____

_____

_____

_____

_____

I WILL CONTEND

"Can the prey be taken from
the mighty man, or the captives
of a tyrant be rescued?"
Surely, thus says the Lord,
"Even the captives of the mighty man
will be taken away, and the prey
of the tyrant will be rescued;
for I will contend with the one
who contends with you,
and I will save your [children]."

–ISAIAH 49:24-25–

NOTES/SCRIPTURES/DATE

_____

_____

_____

THOSE WHO PRAY

Jesus said, "If two of you agree on earth about anything that they may ask, it shall be done for them by My Father who is in Heaven" (Matt. 18:19).

Thus we see that the future of a society does not belong to sinners; it belongs to those who pray.

—IN CHRIST'S IMAGE TRAINING

NOTES/SCRIPTURES/DATE

_____

_____

_____

_____

_____

THE SAME ONE

There is not a different

Jesus in Heaven than He

who dwells in us.

He is Christ wrapped in glory

in Heaven;

He is Christ wrapped in flesh in us.

He is still the One for whom

all things are possible!

—THE DAYS OF HIS PRESENCE

NOTES/SCRIPTURES/DATE

_____

_____

_____

_____

_____

STRATEGY

Our strategy for success in life is
simple: to see what God is doing
and do it, and to hear
what God is saying and say it.

—IN CHRIST'S IMAGE TRAINING

NOTES/SCRIPTURES/DATE

_____

_____

_____

LOVE IS THE FUEL

If we cease to love, we will fail to pray.

Love is the fuel behind all intercession.

—THE POWER OF COVENANT PRAYER

NOTES/SCRIPTURES/DATE

_____

_____

_____

TOO MUCH FAITH?

Step out in faith and observe the concerns people raise to sow doubt. Yes, some concerns should be heeded, but many will be the echo of failures previously experienced by others. "Don't be presumptuous," they will warn. "That didn't work for me," they caution. Of course, we don't want to be presumptuous, but remember: Jesus never warned, "Woe to ye of too much faith." Too much faith hasn't been a problem. Our problem has been believing too little.

—IN CHRIST'S IMAGE TRAINING

NOTES/SCRIPTURES/DATE

_____

_____

_____

_____

_____

COMFORT OR TROUBLE

Through these years in ministry, I have
concluded: Christ comes to comfort
the troubled and trouble the comfortable.

—IN CHRIST'S IMAGE TRAINING

NOTES/SCRIPTURES/DATE

_____

_____

_____

RESCUE THEM

Jesus commanded us to judge not.
He sends us into the world not as judges
of man but, under Him, as co-redeemers.
We are not sent to condemn people
but to rescue them.

—IN CHRIST'S IMAGE TRAINING

NOTES/SCRIPTURES/DATE

_____

_____

_____

THE SECRET PLACE

In God's kingdom the secret
to a successful life before men
is found in the success
of our secret life with God.
Yes, he who finds the secret place
of the Most High and
learns to dwell there
will be successful in all he does.

—IN CHRIST'S IMAGE TRAINING

NOTES/SCRIPTURES/DATE

_____

_____

_____

_____

_____

BY GRACE THROUGH FAITH

Whether our need is for salvation, healing or deliverance, it is always by grace through faith that we advance and find victory. Is there a mountain standing in your way? The Lord would say, "What are you, O great mountain? Before My people you will become a plain. Their spiritual journey will be complete with shouts of 'Grace, grace!'" (Zech. 4:7).

—IN CHRIST'S IMAGE TRAINING ON-SITE SEMINAR

NOTES/SCRIPTURES/DATE

_____

_____

_____

_____

SWEET TASTE OF HOLY FRUIT

There is something winsome, something beautifully attractive, about holiness. When we seek holiness, we are seeking to surround ourselves with the joy of Heaven. To live a holy life is to dwell at the source of all true pleasure. It is to experience life from God's perspective, enjoying life as God Himself would.

—HOLINESS, TRUTH AND THE PRESENCE OF GOD

NOTES/SCRIPTURES/DATE

_____
_____
_____
_____
_____

TOO POLITE?

We have been too polite with God. I do not mean we should be irreverent; I am saying the Lord's Prayer is not a weak, pleading prayer. There is a time to plead with God, but what Jesus gave was prophetic. There is not a "please" in it. Indeed, it's the Father's pleasure to give us His kingdom (Luke 12:32). Thus, Jesus is not instructing us to beg for it, but to align our lives with it and then announce it. He is commanding us to call for God's kingdom to rule on earth, in our lives, churches and cities. This is a prayer of authority. Do we see this? The Son of God wants us to pray like we were created to bring Heaven to earth!

—IN CHRIST'S IMAGE TRAINING

NOTES/SCRIPTURES/DATE

_____

_____

_____

SAME ONENESS

Jesus said, "I am the good shepherd, and I know My own and My own know Me, even as the Father knows Me and I know the Father" (John 10:14–15). Do we grasp this? The very same relational depth enjoyed by the Father and the Son, this same degree of oneness is to be replicated between the Son and us. If we don't enjoy such intimacy now, we should seek God for it. It's waiting.

—IN CHRIST'S IMAGE TRAINING

NOTES/SCRIPTURES/DATE

_____

_____

_____

_____

THE DEVIL KNOWS

The devil knows that if
he can keep our prayers silent,
he keeps God's hand distant.

—IN CHRIST'S IMAGE TRAINING

NOTES/SCRIPTURES/DATE

_____

_____

_____

SET APART

Know that the Lord has set apart
the godly man for Himself.

–PSALM 4:3–

NOTES/SCRIPTURES/DATE

_____

_____

_____

DISPLACING THE FRUIT?

Knowing we would grieve
over the evil in the world,
God's Word tells us,
"Be angry, and yet do not sin"
(Eph. 4:26).
We must discern at what point
our anger about evil
has begun displacing
the fruit of the Spirit in our lives.

—IN CHRIST'S IMAGE TRAINING

NOTES/SCRIPTURES/DATE
_____
_____
_____
_____
_____

THE VERY PASSION

The pattern for leadership

in the years ahead is simple:

leaders must be individuals whose

burning passion is conformity

to Jesus Christ. Is this not

becoming the very passion

of your heart,

to possess the likeness of Christ?

—IN CHRIST'S IMAGE TRAINING

NOTES/SCRIPTURES/DATE

_____

_____

_____

_____

_____

PEACE

The more peace you have

during spiritual attack,

the more truly you are walking

in Christ's victory.

Remember, it is the God of peace

who shall crush Satan

beneath your feet

shortly (Rom. 16:20).

—THE THREE BATTLEGROUNDS

NOTES/SCRIPTURES/DATE

_____

_____

_____

_____

_____

AMBASSADOR

We are called as "ambassadors for Christ" (2 Cor. 5:20; Eph. 6:20). A true ambassador not only represents his or her ruler; an ambassador knows that ruler's policies and how he thinks. He receives regular instruction and thus is current on the leader's goals. Should the ambassador be ignorant of the ruler's view, he does not offer his own opinions; he waits to hear from the one he represents. There are seven billion opinions in the world; the nations are not pining for our opinions, but to hear the words of the One we represent. Ambassador: What is your king speaking today?

—SPIRITUAL DISCERNMENT AND THE MIND OF CHRIST

NOTES/SCRIPTURES/DATE

_____

_____

_____

IN PURSUIT

"[That you may really come] to know [practically, [through experience for yourselves] the love of Christ, which far surpasses mere knowledge [without experience]; that you may be filled [through all your being] unto all the fullness of God [may have the richest measure of the divine Presence, and become a body wholly filled and flooded with God Himself]!" (Eph 3:19 AMP).

Are we seeking to own the "richest measure of the divine Presence"? Are we in pursuit of a life "wholly filled and flooded with God Himself"?

—IN CHRIST'S IMAGE TRAINING

NOTES/SCRIPTURES/DATE

_____

_____

_____

BEING PREPARED

If you find yourself

more drawn toward prayer

than self-promotion,

more toward humility than hype,

you are being prepared

by the Holy Spirit

for the glory of God.

—THE DAYS OF HIS PRESENCE

NOTES/SCRIPTURES/DATE

_____

_____

_____

_____

_____

HIS GOAL

I am convinced that Jesus
not only came to seek and save the lost,
but His goal was to then
replicate Himself in those He saved.

—In Christ's Image Training

NOTES/SCRIPTURES/DATE

_____

_____

_____

GET MY WAY?

The real issue in life is not about
whether I get my way
or you get your way; it's about Yahweh.

—In Christ's Image Training

NOTES/SCRIPTURES/DATE

_____

_____

_____

WITHOUT SIN?

Beware,

Christ's standard

of judgment is high.

He said, "He who is

without sin

among you,

let him be the first

to throw a stone" (John 8:7).

—HOLINESS, TRUTH AND THE PRESENCE OF GOD

NOTES/SCRIPTURES/DATE

_____

_____

_____

_____

_____

GRUMBLING

Paul said that the Israelites who grumbled in the wilderness were "destroyed by the destroyer" (1 Cor. 10:10). Who was this destroyer? Revelation 9:11 says he is king over the bottomless pit; he's the fallen angel ruling the abyss. His name in Hebrew is Abaddon (destruction) and in the Greek, Apollyon (destroyer). My friends, guard your hearts. For when you open the door to grumbling, you open the door to hell.

—THE SHELTER OF THE MOST HIGH

NOTES/SCRIPTURES/DATE

_____

_____

_____

_____

_____

SALVATION

You see, salvation begins with accepting what Jesus did, but it then unfolds until we manifest who Jesus is.

—IN CHRIST'S IMAGE TRAINING

NOTES/SCRIPTURES/DATE

_____

_____

_____

PREPARING YOU

The truth is, the Holy Spirit is preparing you for a new and fresh anointing from the Lord.

—IN CHRIST'S IMAGE TRAINING

NOTES/SCRIPTURES/DATE

_____

_____

_____

SLUMBERING SPIRIT

In the last days, Jesus said there will also be a mysterious drowsiness that we must discern and overcome (Matt. 25:5). This phenomenon of spiritual slumber, of losing our God-seeking hunger, is something we must guard against. When this slumbering spirit approaches, it first dulls our perception. Soon, our zeal for the things of God diminishes. We still love the Lord, but our spiritual vision sits in the back seat as other less important aspects of life set the direction for our lives.

—THE DAYS OF HIS PRESENCE

NOTES/SCRIPTURES/DATE

_____

_____

_____

_____

_____

PEACE EMANATES

Peace is Spirit power. A peace-maker is not merely someone who protests against war; he is one who is inwardly so yielded to Christ in spirit and purpose that he can be called a "son of God" (Matt. 5:9). Where he goes, God goes and where God goes, he goes. He is fearless, calm, and bold. Peace emanates from him the way light and heat radiate from fire.

—THE THREE BATTLEGROUNDS

NOTES/SCRIPTURES/DATE

_____

_____

_____

_____

_____

THE PATTERN

When God said, "Let Us make man in Our image, according to Our likeness" (Gen. 1:26), the image and likeness He had in mind was not Adam; it was Jesus (Rev. 13:8 NKJV; Rom. 8:29; Heb. 2:10). God chose us in Christ before the foundation of the world (Eph. 1:4). Thus, we must see Jesus not only as the payment for our sins but also as the pattern for our lives.

—IN CHRIST'S IMAGE TRAINING

NOTES/SCRIPTURES/DATE

_____

_____

_____

_____

_____

DEPENDENCY

Jesus said that the works He did, we would also do (John 14:12). We assume the word *works* means miracles, but this word (Gk: Ergon) meant "business, employment, that which any one is occupied ... enterprise, undertaking" (Strong's #2041). Because Jesus would dwell in His disciples, He is saying that as we attend to Him, His actual life would reanimate through us. Yes, that includes miracles, but it also includes the less popular works that Jesus did, such as nights in prayer, self-denial, times of fasting, loving sinners, carrying a cross and possessing moment by moment dependency upon God.

—IN CHRIST'S IMAGE TRAINING

NOTES/SCRIPTURES/DATE

_____

_____

_____

THE NECTAR OF TRUTH

We are called to love God with all our heart, all our soul, all our mind; and also to love our neighbors as we love and cherish ourselves (Matt. 22:37–40). Indeed, Jesus tells us that it is through our love for one another that we prove we are truly His disciples. In fact, He calls us to even love our enemies. Here is what I have found: the nectar of truth is love.

—IN CHRIST'S IMAGE TRAINING

NOTES/SCRIPTURES/DATE

_____

_____

_____

_____

_____

DECEIVED

When a person is deceived

he doesn't know

he's deceived,

because he's been deceived.

Therefore we must learn

not merely to be interested

in truth, but to love it.

—THE THREE BATTLEGROUNDS

NOTES/SCRIPTURES/DATE

_____

_____

_____

_____

_____

OUR RESPONSIBILITY

The Almighty not only declares "the end from the beginning" (Isa. 46:10), He has actually created the end from the beginning. "It is done" (Rev. 21:6). Hebrews reveals God's "works were finished from the foundation of the world" (Heb. 4:3). He has already granted us "everything pertaining to life and godliness" (2 Pet. 1:3), and He has already "blessed us with every spiritual blessing in the heavenly places" (Eph. 1:3). Yes, His works unfold in the sequences of time, but it is our responsibility to take God at His Word, to believe that what He has promised He will also bring to pass.

—IN CHRIST'S IMAGE TRAINING

NOTES/SCRIPTURES/DATE

_____

_____

_____

REST

Rest is not in the Sabbath; it is in God. Rest is a prevailing quality of His completeness.

— HOLINESS, TRUTH AND THE PRESENCE OF GOD

NOTES/SCRIPTURES/DATE

_____

_____

_____

CITYWIDE WAR

It takes a citywide church to win the citywide war (Matt. 12:25).

—WHEN THE MANY ARE ONE

NOTES/SCRIPTURES/DATE

_____

_____

_____

IT IS TIME

In the north, the local geese are quiet until the end of summer, but come September the loud honking begins. Flocks crisscross the overhead skies, not only honking to the geese in formation but also calling to the distracted geese still on the ground. It is as though they are saying, "It's time to go! The season is changing. You cannot make the journey alone. Come, join us and fly!" For us, too, the spiritual climate is changing. The call of the Lord's servants is loud and persistent: "The time is at hand. Be not passive nor distracted. For it is time we manifest the glory of Christ!"

—IN CHRIST'S IMAGE TRAINING

NOTES/SCRIPTURES/DATE

_____

_____

_____

_____

CHRIST, OUR ADVOCATE

When the Holy Spirit shows us an area that needs repentance, we must overcome the instinct to defend ourselves. We must silence the little lawyer who steps out from a dark closet in our minds, pleading, "My client is not so bad." This false defense attorney will defend you until the day you die, and if you listen to him you will never see what is wrong in you nor face what you need to change. To grow beyond our preset limitations, the voice of our self-preservation instincts must be muted. For Christ alone is our true advocate.

—THE THREE BATTLEGROUNDS

NOTES/SCRIPTURES/DATE

_____

_____

_____

_____

HEART OF THE CONTRITE

For thus says the high and exalted

One who lives forever,

whose name is Holy,

"I dwell on a high and holy place,

And also with the contrite

and lowly of spirit in order to revive

the spirit of the lowly and to revive

the heart of the contrite."

–ISAIAH 57:15–

NOTES/SCRIPTURES/DATE

_____

_____

_____

_____

_____

LIKE A WATERED GARDEN

CIVILITY

At its essence, the measure of a culture's civilization is revealed in how "civil" people are toward one another, even when they disagree. When we lose civility we become uncivilized. Thus, what is happening in America is shameful. Slander, ranting and accusation have replaced respectful discourse, humility and honor. "Freedom of speech" does not mean freedom to distort, slander and dishonor.

—IN CHRIST'S IMAGE TRAINING

NOTES/SCRIPTURES/DATE

_____

_____

_____

_____

_____

EXCUSE ME?

There are exceptions, but once someone accepts that the only destiny left for their culture is increasing darkness, a deception takes root and grows in their souls. Since they now believe God has turned His back, they too turn their backs and retreat from the front lines of faith and intercession. Indeed, they quietly abandon sacrificing their time and treasure to support strategies to win the lost. In short, once they accept revival is no longer an option in God's heart, they excuse themselves from becoming Christlike.

—IN CHRIST'S IMAGE TRAINING

NOTES/SCRIPTURES/DATE

_____

_____

_____

_____

RESTORED

Satan wants us to believe there exists no hope for our nation and that the time for revival is over. Yes, our world looks dark, but it is not darker than the era of World War I when over 100 nations were engulfed in war and 37 million died. Nor is today more terrifying than the era of World War II when over 70 million died. Next the Cold War arrived with its terrifying threat of nuclear annihilation. The fact is, every generation has had to fight the evil of its time. Let us pray, therefore, and not lose heart. For we too can see righteousness restored to our land.

—IN CHRIST'S IMAGE TRAINING

NOTES/SCRIPTURES/DATE

_____

_____

_____

_____

TRUE LOVE

To all those struggling
with their marriage, don't quit.
Honor your vows and keep God first.
He will show you
what you need to learn.
Above all, forgive each other daily.
True love isn't something you fall into,
it's something you climb to.
There are many rewards for
working through your problems.
Truly, God saves the best for last.

—IN CHRIST'S IMAGE TRAINING

NOTES/SCRIPTURES/DATE

_____

_____

_____

LEADERSHIP FAILED

Jerusalem fell to Babylon during Jeremiah's day for many reasons, but the underlying cause was the apostasy of the religious leaders. The adversary and the enemy entered the gates of the city because of "the sins of her prophets and the iniquities of her priests" (Lam. 4:12–13). Yes, the city was destroyed because the religious leadership failed to bring the people to repentance. They lost the protection of God.

—A House United

NOTES/SCRIPTURES/DATE

_____

_____

_____

_____

HE FIRST LOVED US

God calls us to love Him

with all our heart, mind,

soul and strength

because that is the way

He loves us.

We love because

He first loved us.

—IN CHRIST'S IMAGE TRAINING

NOTES/SCRIPTURES/DATE

_____

_____

_____

_____

_____

LEADS TO HEALING

Repentance precedes
deliverance, and deliverance often
leads to healing in other areas.

—THE THREE BATTLEGROUNDS

NOTES/SCRIPTURES/DATE

_____
_____
_____

HEAVEN PAYS

Heaven pays our tuition,
but it doesn't take our tests.

—IN CHRIST'S IMAGE TRAINING

NOTES/SCRIPTURES/DATE

_____
_____
_____

RESOURCES

Jesus prayed to the Father,

"All things that are Mine are Yours,

and Yours are Mine" (John 17:10).

I read His words to say to me,

"If you turn over

your resources to Me,

I will turn over

My resources to you."

—IN CHRIST'S IMAGE TRAINING

NOTES/SCRIPTURES/DATE

_____

_____

_____

_____

_____

THE WORD

The Word is God.
The Scriptures are not God,
but the Spirit of Truth
that breathes through the words
and makes them alive is
actually God Himself.
And when we read the Sacred Writ,
we should consider
we are gazing through a window
into the heart of God.

—IN CHRIST'S IMAGE TRAINING

NOTES/SCRIPTURES/DATE

_____

_____

_____

I BELIEVE

When Jesus asks, "When the Son of Man comes, will He find faith on the earth?" (Luke 18:8), He is not doubting there will be faith, He is asking us as individuals: Will I find faith in you? We must choose to answer that question in the affirmative. Yes, I believe in You, Lord. I believe You are the same yesterday, today and forever, and that You are the rewarder of those who diligently seek You (Heb. 11:6).

—IN CHRIST'S IMAGE TRAINING

NOTES/SCRIPTURES/DATE

_____
_____
_____
_____

ONLY JUST BEGUN

Beware of spiritual complacency or the subtle sense that you've arrived. I love the prayer of Moses. After he was used by the Lord to deliver Israel from Pharaoh, after he defeated the "gods" of Egypt, after following the pillar of fire and cloud, after seeing the Lord "face to face" in the sacred tent and beholding miracle after miracle for forty years – at the end of his life Moses prayed, "You have begun to show Your servant Your greatness and Your strong hand" (Deut. 3:24). You have begun? No matter how much we attain or experience, let us remember: our journey into God's glory has only just begun.

—I WILL BE FOUND BY YOU

NOTES/SCRIPTURES/DATE

_____

_____

_____

THE BEST FOR LAST

For all those aging folks who feel that time and God have passed them by, let me urge you to fill your last years with prayer. Start a prayer group among your friends. Pray for family, neighbors, cities and nations. Pray that God would send laborers into the harvest, especially to the Muslim world. Regardless of what you think of your political leaders or business leaders or even gang leaders, they only need one touch from God and they will be forever changed. So pray for them! A little forgetful? Then write out your prayers and read them aloud each day. And when you have prayed for all, then pray for me and other church leaders, that we will in all things reveal the person of Jesus Christ. God has saved the best for last!

—IN CHRIST'S IMAGE TRAINING

NOTES/SCRIPTURES/DATE

_____

_____

_____

HE WILL DELIVER

The Holy Spirit has a promise for
those of us who have grown old.
He says, the righteous
"will still bear fruit in old age."
And for those who feel
spiritually dry, again God's Word
promises, you "will stay fresh and green."
With joy, God calls you to proclaim,
"'The Lord is upright;
He is my Rock'" (Ps. 92:12–15 NIV).

—IN CHRIST'S IMAGE TRAINING

NOTES/SCRIPTURES/DATE

_____

_____

_____

TRUST IN HIM

Indeed, as you have done

so many times in your life,

put your trust in the Almighty.

Because you have loved Him,

therefore He will

deliver you! (Ps. 91:14-16)

—IN CHRIST'S IMAGE TRAINING

NOTES/SCRIPTURES/DATE

_____

_____

_____

_____

DREAM DREAMS

I like that Moses was 80 when God appeared to him and that Abraham was in his mid-70s when the Lord first called him. Too many of us reach our 50s and 60s and feel we must surrender God's promises to the next generation. Not so. The promise of the Spirit is that old men will dream dreams – words of divine assignment and fulfillment for their future (Acts 2:17). It's possible the next move of God might just flow out from a prayer meeting in a retirement home somewhere.

—IN CHRIST'S IMAGE TRAINING

NOTES/SCRIPTURES/DATE

_____

_____

_____

_____

GOD'S PLEASURE

There are qualities of heart that actually attract the pleasure of God. If we possess unoffendable faith in our pursuit of Christ's likeness; if we walk humbly with our God; if we position ourselves in the intercessor's gap, and if we abide in Christ-centered unity with our spouse and other local Christians – we will attract the pleasure of God, and when we awaken His pleasure, His power soon follows.

—IN CHRIST'S IMAGE TRAINING

NOTES/SCRIPTURES/DATE

_____

_____

_____

_____

WE THINK WE HAVE

The problem

with many Christians today

is that we have

three quarts of self,

one quart of the Holy Spirit,

and we think we have

a gallon of God.

—IN CHRIST'S IMAGE TRAINING

NOTES/SCRIPTURES/DATE

_____

_____

_____

_____

_____

CONFORMITY

Paul defined intimacy with Christ as the deepest cry of his heart. He wrote, "That I may know Him and the power of His resurrection and the fellowship of His sufferings, being conformed to His death" (Phil. 3:10). Paul was not speaking of some esoteric knowledge of Christ but an intimacy that led to conformity. Do we see this connection? He said, knowing Christ leads to conformity to Christ.

—IN CHRIST'S IMAGE TRAINING

NOTES/SCRIPTURES/DATE

_____

_____

_____

_____

_____

FRAGRANCE

God seeks the revelation
of His Son in us.
There is nothing that so pleases
the Father as when His Son
is revealed through us,
where we crucify our fleshly reactions
so that Christ lives in us
- where we literally become the
"fragrance of Christ
to God" (2 Cor. 2:15).

—IN CHRIST'S IMAGE TRAINING

NOTES/SCRIPTURES/DATE

_____

_____

_____

_____

SENSE WEAKNESSES

One thing I have discovered:
it is when we sense
our weaknesses most vividly
that God can use us most mightily.

—In Christ's Image Training

NOTES/SCRIPTURES/DATE

_____

_____

_____

PIT

The acronym for "prophets

in training" is PIT.

—In Christ's Image Training

NOTES/SCRIPTURES/DATE

_____

_____

_____

WHEN WE PRAY

Each of us knows prayer works.

We are saved today because

someone steadfastly prayed for us.

Thus, looking at the miracle

of our own conversion

we can gain confidence

when we pray for others.

—IN CHRIST'S IMAGE TRAINING

NOTES/SCRIPTURES/DATE

_____

_____

_____

_____

ALWAYS A WAY OUT

When we are born again, Christ enters our lives, not as a religion but as our Redeemer. Yes, He is a prophet; true, He is our teacher. But He is more. In moment-to-moment faithfulness, He is our Savior. We are never on our own, never forced to rely on our own righteousness; never trapped, not even in our mistakes. He works ALL THINGS for our good. Even if we do not see it immediately, there is always a way out of our setbacks. You see, the one great deficiency of all other religions is this: they have no Redeemer.

—IN CHRIST'S IMAGE TRAINING

NOTES/SCRIPTURES/DATE

_____

_____

_____

TO SEE INTO THE UNSEEN

Spiritual discernment is the grace
to see into the unseen.
It is a gift of the Spirit
to perceive the realm of the spirit.

—SPIRITUAL DISCERNMENT AND THE MIND OF CHRIST

NOTES/SCRIPTURES/DATE

_____

_____

_____

A VERY PRESENT HELP

God is our refuge and strength,
A very present help in trouble.

–PSALM 46:1–

NOTES/SCRIPTURES/DATE

_____

_____

_____

GRACE ABOUNDS

Too many of us are so focused on
what the devil is doing that
we fail to see what God is doing.
The primary focus of the Lord
is not on how dark evil is becoming
but how Christlike His people
become! When iniquity abounds,
the grace of God abounds more so.

—THE DAYS OF HIS PRESENCE

NOTES/SCRIPTURES/DATE

_____
_____
_____
_____
_____

DISAPPOINTED?

Are you carrying disappointment in your spirit? Renounce it. Forgive those who have let you down. Have you personally or morally failed? Repent deeply and return to your Redeemer. Disappointment is not just a sad emotional state of mind; deep disappointment actually can sever our hearts from faith. It can "dis-appoint" us from our God-appointed destiny.

—IN CHRIST'S IMAGE TRAINING

NOTES/SCRIPTURES/DATE

_____

_____

_____

_____

A FIT SACRIFICE

At the dedication of the temple the priests fell and could not minister because of the thick, manifest presence of God. Afterward, Solomon, having experienced the living glory, offered 22,000 oxen, 120,000 sheep. When we actually see the glory of God, no sacrifice we bring is enough nor is any time right to end the offering! Indeed, Solomon could have offered a million oxen, yet it would not have satisfied the demands of his own eyes as he beheld God's glory! It is only our deep ignorance of who God actually is that suggests a limit on any sacrifice we offer. Only the inexhaustible sacrifice of Christ, and Christ living through us, makes our offering to God a fit sacrifice.

—HOLINESS, TRUTH AND THE PRESENCE OF GOD

NOTES/SCRIPTURES/DATE

_____

_____

_____

GOD GIVES GRACE

The holiest, most powerful voice that ever spoke described Himself as "meek and lowly in heart" (Matt. 11:29 KJV). Why begin a message on attaining Christlikeness with a quote concerning humility? Simply because spiritual maturity is the product of grace and God gives grace only to the humble.

—HOLINESS, TRUTH AND THE PRESENCE OF GOD

NOTES/SCRIPTURES/DATE

_____

_____

_____

_____

_____

CHOOSE

Our main message at the end of the age is not that judgment and wrath are coming, though both certainly are en route and, even now, the "birth pangs" have begun (Matt. 24:4–8 KJV). Still, our primary message is not that wrath is at hand, but that Heaven is at hand (Matt. 24:14; Dan. 2:44). The nations will receive a genuine opportunity to choose, not between the church and the world but between Heaven and hell, for both will manifest in fullness as the age ends.

—IN CHRIST'S IMAGE TRAINING

NOTES/SCRIPTURES/DATE

_____

_____

_____

LOVE LIKE CHRIST

The effect of being loved by Christ is that we increasingly love like Christ. Has Christ forgiven us? Then we ought to forgive others. Did Christ reach to us while we were yet sinners? Then we ought to reach to sinners. Let us require of ourselves not only to grow in doctrine but to see our knowledge germinate into love.

—In Christ's Image Training

NOTES/SCRIPTURES/DATE

_____

_____

_____

_____

_____

TRANSFORMED

To be transfixed on Christ
is to be transformed by Christ.

—IN CHRIST'S IMAGE TRAINING

NOTES/SCRIPTURES/DATE

_____

_____

_____

THE MERCY PRAYER

We must learn to pray

the mercy prayer:

"Father, forgive them."

—IN CHRIST'S IMAGE TRAINING

NOTES/SCRIPTURES/DATE

_____

_____

_____

I WATER IT

In that day, "A vineyard

of wine, sing of it!

I, the Lord, am its keeper;

I water it every moment.

So that no one will damage it,

I guard it night and day."

–Isaiah 27:2-3–

NOTES/SCRIPTURES/DATE

_____

_____

_____

_____

MY PLEDGE

My attitude is this: I will stand for revival, unity and prayer; I will labor to restore healing and reconciliation between God's people. I will do what I can. Yet, if all God truly wanted was to raise up one fully yielded son – a son who would refuse to be offended, refuse to react, and refuse to harbor unforgiveness regardless of those who slander and persecute – I have determined to be that person. And while I labor to see an awakening in my nation, my primary goal in all things is not revival but first to bring pleasure to Christ.

—THE POWER OF ONE CHRISTLIKE LIFE

NOTES/SCRIPTURES/DATE

_____

_____

_____

_____